D1219927

The Legacy of Michael Sattler

CLASSICS OF THE RADICAL REFORMATION

Cornelius J. Dyck, Editor
Institute of Mennonite Studies

In cooperation with Walter Klaassen, Conrad Grebel College, Waterloo, Ontario; John S. Oyer, Goshen College, Goshen, Indiana; John H. Yoder, Notre Dame University, South Bend, Indiana; and Jarold K. Zeman, Acadia Divinity College, Wolfville, Nova Scotia.

Classics of the Radical Reformation is an English-language series of Anabaptist and free church documents translated and annotated under the direction of the Institute of Mennonite Studies (the research agency of Associated Mennonite Biblical Seminaries, 3003 Benham Avenue, Elkhart, Indiana 46517) and published by Mennonite Publishing House (Herald Press, Scottdale, Pennsylvania 15683).

1. *The Legacy of Michael Sattler.*
    Translated and edited by John H. Yoder, 1973.

2. *The Writings of Pilgram Marpeck.*
    Translated and edited by William Klassen and Walter Klaassen, 1978.

3. *Anabaptism in Outline: Selected Primary Sources.*
    Edited by Walter Klaassen, 1981.

4. *The Sources of Swiss Anabaptism: The Grebel Letters and Related Documents.*
    Edited by Leland Harder, 1985.

5. *Balthasar Hubmaier: Theologian of Anabaptism.*
    Translated and edited by H. Wayne Pipkin and John H. Yoder, 1989.

The Legacy of Michael Sattler

translated
and edited by

John H. Yoder

HERALD PRESS
Scottdale, Pennsylvania
Waterloo, Ontario

Library of Congress Cataloging in Publication Data

Yoder, John Howard, comp.
The Legacy of Michael Sattler.

(Classics of the radical Reformation, 1)
Bibliography; p.
1. Theology — Collected works — 16th century
2. Anabaptists — Collected works. I. Sattler,
Michael, d. 1527. II. Title. III. Series.
BX4929.Y6   1973   284'.3   72-6333
ISBN 0-8361-1187-7

Photos by Jan Gleysteen, from the Anabaptist Heritage Collection, Goshen, Indiana.

THE LEGACY OF MICHAEL SATTLER
Copyright © 1973 by Herald Press, Scottdale, Pa. 15683
    Published simultaneously in Canada by Herald Press,
    Waterloo, Ont. N2L 6H7. All rights reserved.
Library of Congress Catalog Card Number: 72-6333
International Standard Book Number: 0-8361-1187-7
Printed in the United States of America
Design by Jan Gleysteen

97 96 95 94 93 92 91 90 89 10 9 8 7 6 5 4

General Editors' Preface

For many years a committee of European and North American historians known as the *Täuferaktenkommission* has been guiding the publication of source materials from the sixteenth-century Anabaptist movement in the original languages under the title *Quellen zur Geschichte der Täufer.* While these sources continue to be the indispensable tool of the specialist they remain largely inaccessible to the growing number of students, churchmen, and lay readers who do not read German or Dutch, except for the available translations of the writings of Menno Simons, Dirk Philips, and Peter Riedemann, the collection prepared by Professor George H. Williams of Harvard University for the *Library of Christian Classics*, Volume 25, the century-old version of the *Martyrs Mirror,* and a handful of other documents.

The intention of the *Classics of the Radical Reformation* series, therefore, is to make available in the English language a scholarly and critical edition of the primary works of major Anabaptist and Free Church writers of the sixteenth and seventeenth centuries. It has not been considered essential to the purposes of the series to include every known document of the writers under translation, nor to pursue text-critical issues at length, unless this contributes to a fuller understanding of the substance of the text, since scholars interested in these details would be forced to turn to the original language text in any case. Where a choice had to be made between clarity and awkward literalism, the translators were encouraged to favor readability without compromising the text.

Translators and editors are at work on subsequent volumes

in the series. The next to appear will be *The Writings of Pilgram Marpeck* translated and edited by William Klassen and Walter Klaassen. Clarence Bauman is preparing a volume on Hans Denck. Additonal books will deal with the writings of Andreas Karlstadt, Dirk Philips, Balthasar Hubmaier, and the Czech Reformation.

It is appropriate to express appreciation to the translators-editors for their labors which were, for the most part, done on their own time. The counsel of the North American Committee for the Documentation of Free Church Origins (NACDFCO), of which Professor George H. Williams serves as chairman, Professor Walter Klaassen as secretary, and Professor Franklin H. Littell as treasurer, is also gratefully acknowledged, as is the help and encouragement of the late Professor Carl S. Meyer, director of the Foundation for Reformation Research, St. Louis, Missouri. This series could not have been undertaken without the commitment of Mennonite Publishing House to the work of the church and its willingness to include it as part of its total responsibility to church and society.

The Institute of Mennonite Studies
Cornelius J. Dyck, Director
John H. Yoder, Associate Director

Preface

The radical edge of the Reformation of the sixteenth century, variously referred to by its contemporaries as "fanatic" or as "anabaptist," was a vast and variegated movement, borrowing freely from many sources in pre-Reformation mysticism, in pre-Reformation dissent, in renaissance humanism, and in the Protestant Reformation.

That there could arise within this movement of such great diversity the organizing principles of believers' baptism and the structuring of the visible congregation was, however, not a fortuitous fallout, but was rather the work of a specific circle of young men near the center of the Zwinglian Reformation, building upon the congregationalist theology of the early Zwingli.

That through the continuing turbulence there could develop a structured movement capable of surviving without the support of the state, was the work largely of the literary and organizational leadership of men of the second generation: Menno Simons in the North, Pilgram Marpeck in the South, Peter Riedemann in the East.

But between these two stages there needed to be a bridge. That Anabaptism survived as a viable movement with visible structures from the naive beginnings in Zürich in the mid 1520s to the time of the synthesizers of the 1540s, was the work of Michael Sattler more than any other one person and was the effect of the *Seven Articles of Schleitheim*, more than any other one single cause. It is this transition between birth and consolidation which is documented by the present collection of materials.

This collection is hereby dedicated to John Christian

7

Wenger, who first translated most of these materials and has had the most to do with the growth of our present understanding of the significance of Sattler. Gratitude is also due to Mr. Nelson Springer, curator of the Mennonite Historical Library at Goshen, to Dr. Myron S. Augsburger, who on the basis of perspective acquired during his preparation of a dissertation on Michael Sattler shared with J. C. Wenger the function of editorial consultant; to Dr. Heinold Fast for advanced communication of the newly edited Schleitheim text, and to Dr. Hans-Jürgen Goertz for assistance in the preparation of the map. Dr. Fast and Studienrat Oskar Wedel were of assistance with clarification of linguistic points. The Institute of Mennonite Studies was generous in the provision of secretarial services.

John H. Yoder
Elkhart, Indiana

Abbreviations

ADB — Allgemeine Deutsche Biographie

ARG — Archiv für Reformationsgeschichte

BRN — Bibliotheca Reformatoria Neerlandica

CR — Corpus Reformatorum

ME — Mennonite Encyclopedia

MGB — Mennonitische Geschichtsblätter

ML — Mennonitisches Lexikon

MQR — Mennonite Quarterly Review

RPTK — Realencyklopädie für protestantische Theologie und Kirche (Herzog-Hauck)

MS — Leonhard von Muralt und Walter Schmid, eds., Quellen zur Geschichte der Täufer in der Schweiz, Bd. I, Hirzel Verlag, Zürich, 1952.

SAW — George H. Williams and Angel Mergal, Spiritual and Anabaptist Writers, Library of Christian Classics, Vol. XXV, Philadelphia, 1957.

Z — Huldreich Zwingli's Sämmtliche Werke

Contents

Introduction

A. In Lieu of a Biography

Michael Sattler was born sometime around 1490 at Stauffen in the Breisgau. He entered the Benedictine Monastery of St. Peter's, northeast of Freiburg, where he became — or was likely to become — prior. In the 1520s he came, by way of Lutheran and Zwinglian ideas, to forsake the monastery and to marry, and by March, 1525, had become a member of the Anabaptist movement which had just begun at Zürich two months before.[1]

Although his major focus of activity probably continued to be in the Breisgau, Sattler was again at Zürich for the great disputation of November 6-8, 1525, following which he was imprisoned and then expelled on November 18.[2] He continued active in Breisgau and Württemberg until we find him a year later in Strasbourg.

With these few lines we have sketched practically all that is known of the life of Sattler up until the time of the earliest documents in the present collection. The story of the six months he had left to live, to the extent that we may seek to reconstruct it, is told below in the introductory comments to each of the documents. It is not the intention of this book to supersede any of the existing biographies of Sattler[3] nor to fill in the many remaining gaps.[4]

Michael Sattler has been called by both admirers and critics the most significant of the first-generation leaders of Anabaptism.[5] The testing of this description, as well as any further description of his stature and character, will best be permitted to arise out of the documents themselves.

Stauffen im Breisgau, birthplace of Michael Sattler.

St. Peter in the Black Forest, the Benedictine monastery of which Michael Sattler was prior.

B. Principles of Translation and Annotation

All of the material in the present volume has been re-translated. After the preparation of our own first draft translation, the extant translations (in most cases by Prof. J. C. Wenger, who is chiefly responsible for Sattler's coming more widely to American historians' attention) were consulted and where their rendering was found equally valid, it was used in preference to our own first draft. Thus in effect, despite the independent beginning, these translations can also in a sense be thought of as an extensive revision of the earlier ones. At a few points, the changes made are identified and the reasons for them indicated; not so much with pedantic intent, as because difficulties and differences in the judgments of translators are often a key to issues of content and interpretation.

The translation is moderately literal; where a choice was necessary between precision of rendering and literary smoothness in English, the former was preferred. The second person singular has been rendered by "you" and "your" except for references to Deity.

Scripture references are reproduced in the body of the text only if they were present in the original. No effort has been made to reproduce the variety of ways in which these citations were identified typographically. Sometimes they appear in the original in parentheses and sometimes without; sometimes with chapter numbers in numerals and sometimes in words; sometimes in the text and sometimes in the margin.

Identification of scriptural allusions is provided in the footnotes only if this has been suggested already by earlier commentators or if the allusion is not immediately visible as such in translation. As reprints succeeded one another in the sixteenth century, the number of textual references in the margin increased progressively. The 1560 Dutch printing has references in the margin at the rate of nearly one per line of text. No effort has been made to reproduce these further references.

Biographical and historical annotation is limited to what might throw light on the meaning of the text or the stature of Sattler's personage. Details of date, the sequence of events, cross-relation of documents and sources are not pursued.

The annotation claims no completeness. German sources are generally not cited where their substance has been reworked in English (i.e., the substance of several biographical articles by Bossert, Hein, Wiswedel is taken up into the biography of *ME*). German sources cited in the secondary literature but inaccessible in Indiana have not been verified (especially with regard to the details of Sattler's imprisonment and trial).

C. *History of Texts and Prints*

The earliest printing of any of the material in this collection was Klaus von Graveneck's account of the martyrdom of Sattler (Item IV in the present volume), which must have been printed within a few weeks of Sattler's death.[6] From this source it was translated into the Dutch in a form which was to be printed in numerous martyrologies, beginning with *Het Offer des Heeren* (1562).[7]

Huldreich Zwingli translated portions of the *Schleitheim Seven Articles* (our Item II), in the process of refuting it and another Anabaptist text, in his *Contra Catabaptistarum Strophas Elenchus*, of August 1527. At the time of writing, Zwingli had four manuscript copies of this text in hand;[8] his translation is the first printed witness to the existence of the *Seven Articles*.[9]

Two early pamphlets are closely related. One of them (which we henceforth shall call A) contains the seven articles (II), the letter to Horb (III), and a somewhat briefer account of the martyrdom (IV) and bears no date.[10] The second (which we shall refer to as text B) contains the same items and in addition the tract on divorce (VI), at the end of which the date 1533 is indicated. Walter Köhler, who reprinted B, argues[11] that it is the earlier of the two, on the basis of his impression that the slight textual differences be-

13

tween the two betray editorial "smoothing out" in the undated edition. This argument is hardly conclusive; the changes
could also be corruptions or corrections introduced by the
second typesetter. When pamphlets like this were reprinted
they were more often changed by the increase of their contents, than by abbreviation. According to this consideration
the addition of the divorce tract to the imprint B would
argue for the priority of the undated pamphlet A. Böhmer[12]
who reprinted the *Seven Articles* alone from text A, assumes without argument its priority. For our purposes the
differences are not significant. Our translation is based upon
the Köhler reprint, except for the *Seven Articles*, where we
have established our own German text. From these two
nearly identical pamphlets, their substance went into the manuscript tradition of the Hutterian Brethren, in which they can
be found recopied numerous times.[13] We shall consider
none of the Hutterian manuscript material as providing an
independent textual tradition.

A French translation of some of this material was
prepared and printed no later than 1544, when an answer to
it was written by John Calvin.[14] It was circulated from
Bonneville (now called La Neuveville, in the canton of
Neuchatel) at the instigation of an Anabaptist in that area
named Pelloux or Pelot. Thence it was sent to Calvin by
reformed pastors in Bonneville.[15] Calvin quoted only brief
portions of the *Seven Articles*, and agrees with the major
substance of three of them. The original print from which Calvin quotes has completely disappeared. Since Calvin in his
concluding comments refers to a report of the "martyrdom of
some Michael," we know that in addition to the *Seven Articles*
at least the martyrdom account was in the translation. One
might surmise that it may well have been based on print A or
B above. Calvin's polemic was translated into English and into
Latin;[16] thus the first English translation of any portion of
the Schleitheim material was the one which had passed
through the French. Calvin says it was printed "In Germany";
probably the German-speaking part of Switzerland.

There is preserved in the Mennonite Historical Library at Goshen, Indiana, a *Sammelband*,[17] the second half of which contains most of the texts of our present collection, inserting the satisfaction tract (our Item VII) before the one on divorce (VI), in addition to two texts from Melchior Rinck. It is from this print that the translations of items VII to IX in the present collection have been prepared. This collection was printed as a unit together with a topical concordance. From internal evidence[18] we can surmise with relative certainty that this was not the first printing of this collection of texts relating to Sattler and Rinck. It might be supposed that in the earlier printing the tract materials were independent of the concordance. The printing would most likely have been done prior to 1560, when the same set of materials appeared in Dutch. There was another reprint sometime in the seventeenth century with the addition of the hymn (Item XI/A).[19]

In 1560 and again about 1565 this same collection of materials was printed in Dutch translation. According to Professor S. Cramer, who edited these materials,[20] the various texts show linguistic signs of having been translated at different times and by different persons. They are not in the same sequence as in the German; nevertheless the present combined form is the earliest known printing of any of them.

The tract, *How Scripture Should Be Discerningly Exposited*, has a completely separate textual history, of which little is known, cf. below pages 150 ff.

Notes

1. The first sign of Sattler's Anabaptist connections is in two documents, found on the same sheet of paper in the Zürich archives. The first records the positions taken by seventeen Anabaptists who were held captive after a hearing or "disputation" on Monday, March 20, 1525. During this hearing they were brought one by one before a group composed of the three city preachers (Zwingli, Jud, Engelhart), three heads of monastic houses, three *Bürgermeisters*, three other members of the city Council, and two schoolmasters. Then their responses were separately recorded. Six held firm against infant baptism, one equivocated, and the rest all were ready to recant. Sattler comes fifteenth on the list, just after Felix Mantz and George Blaurock:

"Brother (*Michael*) [another hand] in the white coat is ready to desist from rebaptism, and has now learned sufficiently, that he confesses having done wrong, and will recant his doctrine, which he preached concerning baptism, etc."

These responses were reported to the Council Saturday 25 March. The second document is the Council's ruling on the fines and the form of recantation which would be required. The Council expelled all the foreigners whether they recanted or not: "Concerning the foreigners, namely Peter Forster, schoolmaster from Luzern, Gabriel Giger from St. Gall, Valentin Gredig from Savoy, Hans Bichtler from Walmenschwil, George from Chur, called Blaurock, and the brother in the white coat, called (*Michael*), [another hand], it is decided, that they shall swear immediately out of milords' jurisdiction and territory and [swear to] their will no more hither, etc."

Some time after this council ruling, the name "Michael" was inserted by another hand in the gaps in the texts, and on the margin was added: "has sworn out" (*vMS* Nos. 62, 64, 65, pp. 70-72). To "swear out" is to promise by oath to leave a given territory.

2. The November "Great Disputation" at Zürich was called to quiet the complaints of the Anabaptist leaders, who found sympathetic listeners, especially in the Grüningen countryside, that they had not really been given a chance to have their convictions tested by the Bible (cf: J. H. Yoder, *Die Gespräche Zwischen Täufern und Reformatoren in der Schweiz 1523-1538*, Karlsruhe, 1962, pp. 69 ff.). Grebel, Mantz, and Blaurock were already prisoners; others of the Anabaptist spokesmen as far as we know, were taken prisoner because they had come, voluntarily, to the gathering. On November 18 the council ruled that the three ringleaders should be held in prison, and that the release of the two others was to depend on their willingness to recant (for the woman from Zürich) or to promise to leave (Ulrich Teck of Waldshut). Sattler agreed to swear that he would never return to Zürich: "Marthy Ling from Schaffhausen and Michael Sattler from Stauffen in Breisgau shall be released upon *Urfehde* and costs." *Urfehde* is the oath of renunciation (*vMS* No. 133, p. 136). Originally it meant a promise to renounce vengeance (*Fehde*: feud or feudal oath); by the sixteenth century it had come to include other kinds of renunciation; here specifically a promise to leave the country, or to cease associating with Anabaptists. It has been suggested by Ds. H. W. Meihuizen (*MQR*, XLI, 1967, p. 207) that Sattler might be the same monk mentioned in a letter from Hans Künzi von Klingnau to the Zürich Council, of whom it is said that he was not yet baptized (*vMS* No. 182, p. 201). Meihuizen suggests that this might explain why Sattler was willing both in March and in November to swear the *Urfehde*. This hypothesis is unlikely. Künzi's account is undatable and he furthermore denies that the unbaptized monk who came to him was the same as "the Michel who was previously your prisoner." Sattler's willingness to swear is more easily explained otherwise: (a) the rejection of the oath was the least clear of the Anabaptist distinctives in 1525; (b) it was not a clear common conviction of the Anabaptists, even later, that the *Urfehde* was identical with the swearing which Jesus and James forbid; and (c) Anabaptists, being human, sometimes weakened under persecution. Later Anabaptists understood the *Urfehde* as sin not because it was an oath but because it was a denial of the faith; but it was a sin which the congregation could forgive, restoring the momentarily unfaithful brother to fellowship, and releasing him from the promise he had made (Yoder, *Gespräche*, p. 126).

3. The standard biographical outline is that of G. Bossert, adapted by H. S. Bender in *ME*, IV, 427 ff. A fictionalized version has been written by Myron Augsburger, *Pilgrim Aflame*, Scottdale, 1967. The only other biography which is significantly independent of Bossert is Wiswedel, *Bilder und Führergestalten aus dem Täufertum*, Vol. III, Kassel, 1952, pp. 9-23.

4. We have made no effort to run down the numerous biographical and bibliographical leads which might throw a little more light on Sattler and his fate. Many of the sources would not be accessible in North America, especially those dealing with the trial proceedings, and what could be learned from them would little change the picture of Sattler which his writings give.

5. In this context the "first generation" must mean those leaders whose major contribution was made by 1527. Several such testimonies are cited below pp. 19f, 47f. Cf. also "Sattler's Abiding Contribution in Anabaptist-Mennonite Theology" in Myron S. Augsburger, *Michael Sattler, d. 1527, Theologian of the Swiss Brethren Movement,* unpublished dissertation, Union Theological Seminary, Richmond, 1965, p. 214.

6. It is referred to as "a printed booklet" in the *Faithful Warning* of Martin Bucer and Wolfgang Capito, the writing of which was concluded July 2, 1527. Manfred Krebs und Hans Georg Rott, *Quellen zur Geschichte der Täufer,* Elsass, 1-Teil, Band VII, 1959, p. 110, also reprinted by Stupperich (see below, p. 24, note 4).

7. Samuel Cramer, *Het Offer des Herren,* 's Gravenhage, 1904, p. 62. BRN II The only non-Dutch materials in *Het Offer* are the martyrdom of Stephen, quoted directly from Acts 6 and 7, and the Sattler account.

8. Cf. below, p. 32.

9. It was also from Zwingli that the first full translation into English was made. Cf. below, p. 33, note 18.

10. The date 1527 appears on the title page, but this is as part of the title of the martyrdom account, and not necessarily the date of printing.

11. Clemen, Otto, and Köhler, Walter, *Flugschriften aus den ersten Jahren der Reformation (Band 2, Heft 3),* Leipzig, 1908, p. 300.

12. Heinrich Böhmer, *Urkunden zur Geschichte des Bauernkrieges und der Wiedertäufer,* Berlin, 1933, pp. 25 ff.

13. Their distribution is surveyed by Robert Friedmann, "The Schleitheim Confession (1527) and other Doctrinal Writings of the Swiss Brethren in a Hitherto Unknown Edition," *MQR,* XVI, 1942, p. 86.

14. "Brieve instruction pour armer tous bons fideles . . ." *CR,* VII, pp. 45-142.

15. Maurice Dumont, *Les Anabaptistes en Pays Neuchatelois,* licentiate thesis at Neuchatel, 1937, pp. 7-10. Pelot or Pelloux was the brother-in-law of the leader of the Protestant community of the parish of Cornaux. Both of them were banished sometime in early 1543, but the issue of infant baptism continued to make difficulty for the Calvinist pastors of the region. It was through them that the request reached John Calvin for his assistance in refutation. These troubles were the occasion of the promulgation by the governor general of Neuchatel, George de Rive, of an edict against Anabaptism (Dumont, p. 11). Ignoring the material reported by Dumont, Irvin B. Horst speculates at some length in his *The Radical Brethren: Anabaptism and the English Reformation to 1558* (Nieuwkoop, de Graaf, 1972), pp. 185 ff., about whether an English translation of the Schleitheim text might be the otherwise not identifiable "books of Anabaptist confession" seized by the English police sometime before 1536, and whether Calvin's "Short instruction" might have been written for the sake of English inquirers. The entire argument is based on the assumption that "evidence is lacking" for a French translation, and on the further strained assumption that Netherlandish Melchiorites in the 1530s would be circulating a Swiss Brethren confession of which there is otherwise no evidence in the Netherlands until after 1550. Calvin's preface refers to the presence of William Farel in Neuchatel and to Farel's debate with Pelot in Bonneville.

16. John Calvin, *A Short Instruction for to Arme all Good Christian People Against the Pestiferous Errours of the Common Sect of the Anabaptists,* London, 1549; the Latin translation was printed in 1552 as part of *Joannis Calvini opuscula omnia in unum volumen collecta* (Geneva).

17. Robert Friedmann, *loc. cit.,* p. 82.

18. The Dutch text preserves at one point a correct reading, of which the equivalent in this volume is corrupted. The Dutch text must then necessarily be based upon an uncorrupted and therefore an earlier printing. Cf. below, p. 127, note 4.

19. Friedmann, *loc. cit.,* p. 87.

20. Cramer, *BRN,* V. 1909, pp. 583 ff.; the textual analysis of the likely history of translation of each tract is given on p. 586.

I

Parting with the Strasbourg Reformers

Introduction

Sometime in 1526 Michael Sattler came to Strasbourg and visited there with the leading Reformer Martin Bucer and his colleague Wolfgang Capito,[1] the most friendly toward the Anabaptists of all the Reformers. The city of Strasbourg was as well the most tolerant of the city states of southern Germany and Switzerland.

These weeks in Strasbourg must have been full of movement, whose meaning we can only partially reconstruct from the records. Hans Denck, Ludwig Hätzer, and Sattler were there at the same time. When Denck and Sattler are contrasted, it is clear that Sattler was closer to Bucer and Capito; Denck was obliged to leave the city by council action on 24 December, 1526, at the same time that Sattler stayed on.[2] The present text seems even at the outset to indicate that Sattler's decision to leave was his own; that he might even have had some thought of staying in Strasbourg — one must wonder with what status.

Ludwig Hätzer on the other hand stayed on when Sattler left. Bucer later says that Hätzer "claimed when with us (though he had shown himself otherwise in Zürich before) to be no Anabaptist. After a conversation with him he called Michael Sattler a 'shrewd and wicked rascal, from whom he had hoped for something better.' He praised God that we left baptism free.[3] Said that if others had dealt with the matter as we did, this error would not have spread so far."[4] From this it would seem that Hätzer was closer to the Reformers than was Sattler, who in turn was closer to them than Denck. Yet in early February Hätzer, in turn, had to leave Strasbourg,[5] and joined Denck in Worms.

Sattler seems not to have been involved in the debates and informal discussions held by the Reformers with Hans Denck, which culminated in a public debate December 22 and in Denck's forced departure.[6] A *Faithful Warning*, published in July 1527 by Bucer and Capito, directly attacking Hans Denck and Jacob Kautz, has only good things to say about Sattler. The Reformers thus clearly held him in another category from those other Anabaptists:

> But we do believe that God also let some of His own come into such an error. Thus we do not doubt that Michael Sattler, who was burned at Rottenburg, was a dear friend of God, even though he was a leader in the baptism order;[7] yet much more qualified and honorable than some others. He also spoke concerning baptism, in such a way that you can see that he only rejected that infant baptism, through which one thinks to be saved. For, as a printed booklet concerning him reports, he proved his point by arguing that faith alone can save. Furthermore he pled for instruction from biblical Scripture and offered to accept the same. Therefore we do not doubt that he is a martyr of Christ. Saint Cyprian, likewise also Tertullian and many others have also always been held by everyone to have been holy martyrs, and have nevertheless held to serious errors. Still with regard to the redemption of Christ, upon which everything depends, we have found no such error in this Michael Sattler as in Denck.[8]

A fuller testimony to the respect which the two Strasbourg Reformers held for Sattler will be found in the Capito letters (Items V A and B below). A more critical report was made by Jacob Ottelin, pastor in Lahr across the Rhine, where Sattler presumably was active just after leaving Strasbourg. Since it is the only clearly negative statement on record concerning Sattler's character we should in fairness reproduce the portion of this letter which refers to him.[9]

> Especially prominent in this movement is that Michael who was formerly a monk at St. Peter's; the most stiff-necked of all. He

makes concessions to no one,[10] condemns all magistracy, and will not flatter anyone for a hair,[11] even for a moment, even when love demands it. Rather he always attacks, in a terrifying way with battle cries, the one who has been called up because of his effrontery[12] and also whoever criticizes the monasticism[13] of his position. He crawls all over anyone who brings him Scripture, calling them disciples of the dead letter. In the place of scriptural proof he claims that the Spirit has, by a simple gesture, revealed to him everything which needs to be believed. With his own spirit he distorts according to his opinion the particular things which are to be proved.[14]

The Bossert-Bender biography called this first document, the letter from Sattler to the Strasbourg Reformers, "A summary of Anabaptist teaching after consultation with the Anabaptists of Strasbourg." This would suggest to the reader that Sattler, in consultation with his brothers and sisters, wrote about Anabaptist distinctives such as baptism, communion, the sword, the oath, etc. . . . But such topics are not the subject of the present text. Its twenty theses are rather a statement of Sattler's hermeneutic foundation, underlying all his particular convictions.

A more direct reading of the text would rather suggest a full reconstruction of the sequence of events:

Sattler first laid before Bucer and Capito (probably orally) his views on baptism, communion, the sword, the oath, the ban. . . .[15] He designates this as what "I together with my brothers and sisters have understood out of Scripture"; this phrasing is not in reference to a particular consultation with Anabaptists in Strasbourg, but rather as a testimony to the general Anabaptist consensus on these matters;

Bucer and Capito had rejected these positions by constant recourse to the theme "love is the end of the law," undercutting by means of one proof text (1 Tim. 1:5) the rigorous application of any New Testament imperatives;[16]

Sattler now sets down his own hermeneutic understanding, whereby he sees scriptural imperatives as not undermined but undergirded by grace.

The Bossert-Bender text goes on to say that this letter "shows a mystical-quietistic piety, but at the same time a deep inwardness and holy earnestness." It is not evident from the text as we have it wherein it smacks of mysticism or quietism. It is a part of a serious conversation with Christian brethren about Christian obedience. Both the concern for the brethren and the concern for obedience to the commands of Scripture distinguish it from what is usually called mystical or quietistic. Bossert was probably misled here by a misinterpretation of the concept of *Gelassenheit:* see in the text below p. 26 note 41.

These twenty theses are all direct New Testament quotations or allusions,[17] most of them rephrased or pointed up to relate to the question at issue. A few of the early ones allude directly to baptism and a few toward the end to the sword; but even these serve not as proof texts but as theological generalizations.

Two overlapping themes dominate this list: solidarity with Christ whereby the Christian's life becomes an outworking of the divine nature; and the polarity Christ/Belial dividing all mankind, making history the arena of combat between two camps. While these themes are fully compatible with the Anabaptist thought which went before Sattler,[18] their concentrated clarity and the light they throw on all his thought are new. They may owe something to the devotional heritage of the Benedictines.[19]

The Text

Michael Sattler to his beloved brothers in God Capito and Bucer and others who love and confess Christ from the heart.[20]

Grace and peace from God our Father through Jesus Christ our Savior. Dear brothers in God! As I recently spoke with you in brotherly moderation and friendliness on several points, which I together with my brothers and sisters have understood out of Scripture, namely out of the New Testament,[21] and you for your part as the ones asked answered in similar moderation and friendliness as follows: Paul writes in 1 Timothy 1[22] that love is the end of the commandment, wherefore it is necessary that all of the commands of God be guided by the same — I am not able so to conceive, in my understanding and conscience, that this may be done[23] as you do it with every point; namely with baptism, the Lord's Supper, force or the sword, the oath, the ban, and all the commandments of God. What hinders me is the following:

1. Christ came to save all of those who would believe in Him alone.[24]

2. He who believes and is baptized will be saved; he who does not believe will be damned.[25]

3. Faith in Jesus Christ reconciles us with the Father and gives us access to Him.[26]

4. Baptism incorporates all believers into the body of Christ, of which He is the head.[27]

5. Christ is the head of His body, i.e., of the believers or the congregation.[28]

6. As the head is minded, so must its members also be.[29]

7. The foreknown and called believers shall be conformed to the image of Christ.[30]

8. Christ is despised in the world.[31] so are also those who are His;[32] He has no kingdom in the world,[33] but that which is of this world is against His kingdom.[34]

9. Believers are chosen out of the world, therefore the world hates them.[35]

10. The devil is prince over the whole world, in whom all the children of darkness rule.[36]

11. Christ is Prince of the Spirit, in whom all who walk in the light live.[37]

12. The devil seeks to destroy, Christ seeks to save.[38]

13. The flesh is against the spirit and the spirit against the flesh.[39]

14. Those who are spiritual are Christ's; those who are

carnal belong to death and to the wrath of God.[40]

15. Christians are fully yielded and have placed their trust in their Father in heaven without any outward or worldly arms.[41]

16. The citizenship of Christians is in heaven and not on earth.[42]

17. Christians are the members of the household of God and fellow citizens of the saints, and not of the world.[43]

18. But they are the true Christians who practice in deed the teaching of Christ.[44]

19. Flesh and blood, pomp and temporal, earthly honor and the world cannot comprehend the kingdom of Christ.[45]

20. In sum: There is nothing in common between Christ and Belial.[46]

Such considerations, and still much more of the same kind, which do not now come to mind, hinder me, dear brothers, from understanding[47] your general assertion on every subject which you advocate with the words of Paul cited above. Therefore, my beloved in God, I know of no comfort in all despair except to address an humble prayer to God the Father for you and for me, that He might be willing to teach us in all truth by His Spirit. Herewith I commend you to the Lord, for as I understand it, I can no longer remain here without doing a special dishonor to God; therefore I must for the sake of my conscience leave the field to the opposition.[48] I beg you herein, that you understand this as an act of Christian humility on my part. The Lord will ultimately dispose.[49]

Be mercifully considerate, I pray you, of those who are in prison and do not permit a merciful judgment to be superseded by a blind, spiteful, and cruel one. Those who are in error[50] (if that they were) are not to be coerced but after a second admonition to be avoided. Christians admonish benevolently, out of sympathy and compassion for the sinful, and do not legalistically coerce persons this way or that.[51] May the Lord God have mercy on us all and give us His Spirit to lead us in the way, Christ Jesus, through whom we can again come into our kingdom, fatherland, and citizenship. Amen. The Lord be with you all dear brothers in God. Amen.

Michael Sattler, your brother in God the heavenly Father.

Notes

1. According to C. Gerbert, *Geschichte der Strassburger Sectenbewegung zur Zeit der Reformation 1524-1534,* Strasbourg, 1889, p. 49, Sattler was a guest in Capito's home. Gerbert does not indicate whether this is a probable surmise (since Capito often welcomed travelers into his home) or a documented certainty. In any case we cannot say that there was already at this time an established Anabaptist congregation with whose members Sattler would rather have stayed.

2. Walter Fellmann, *Hans Denck: Schriften* (Teil II), Gütersloh, 1956, p. 14; Krebs-Rott, *op. cit.,* Nos. 64-66, pp. 60-62.

3. I. e., that we did not legally enforce infant baptism and thereby make Anabaptism a civil crime.

4. These words are near the close of the *Faithful Warning,* Krebs-Rott, *loc. cit.,* p. 114, and Robert Stupperich, *Martin Bucer's Deutsche Schriften* (Band II), Gütersloh, 1962, p. 258.

5. J. F. Gerhard Goeters, *Ludwig Hätzer, Spiritualist und Antitrinitarier,* Gütersloh, 1957, p. 95.

6. Even though he was not involved in these police actions against Denck, it might still be that they were the occasion for Sattler's conversation with the Reformers which resulted in the present document.

7. The label "Baptism Order," *(Tauforden)* was a favorite early critics' designation for the Anabaptists. It included the reproach of self-righteous legalism, carrying over from the Protestant rejection of the monastic orders, as well as the identification of a small circle voluntarily adhering to a distinct rule of life.

8. Krebs-Rott, *op. cit.,* No. 86, p. 110; also in Stupperich, p. 253.

9. Letter of 7 February 1527 from Ottelin or Oettli to Martin Bucer, Krebs-Rott, *op. cit.,* No. 75, p. 73. Assistance in the interpretation of this letter was received from Studienrat O. Wedel.

10. Alternative translation: "He respects no one."

11. This reference to hair might mean that Sattler is not properly respectful of the aged; of gray hair; or it might rather mean "not by the breadth of a hair," not the least bit.

12. If taken literally, a person who "has been called up because of his effrontery" would seem to be an individual subject to some kind of moral admonition or church discipline, earning a reprimand but whom Sattler is accused of scolding too severely. An alternative less literal translation could refer instead to someone "whom his [Sattler's] effrontery has accused."

13. Cf. note 7 above.

14. This phrase might refer either to positions of his own which Sattler is supporting with scriptural argument or to those of his opponents from whom he demands scriptural support: in either case Oettli believes that in the process of argument Sattler does violence to the texts, and that this is connected to Sattler's appeal to the Holy Spirit. This is, in any case, a testimony against classifying Sattler as a biblical literalist.

15. The choice of items at issue, and even much of their sequence, is strikingly

parallel to that we shall observe later at Schleitheim.

16. This was not Capito's only argument, though it may have been the predominant one in the debating situation. Some other arguments are indicated in Capito's letter to the Church at Horb (below pp. 71 ff.).

17. *ME*, IV, p. 428, ignores the textual base and thereby suggests the "theses" were Sattler's own.

18. If we consider Sattler as having settled his Anabaptist allegiance and beliefs by late summer of 1525, there is a very limited body of literature testifying to the sources from which he could have borrowed: (a) The oral tradition of the first Swiss Brethren, as testified to in the Grebel letter to Müntzer of September, 1524, Geo. H. Williams and A. Mergal, *Spiritual and Anabaptist Writers*, LCC, Vol. XXV, Philadelphia, 157, pp. 71 ff. (hereafter known as SAW); (b) The earliest collections of arguments on baptism, of which several are known (Heinold Fast, "Hans Krüsis Büchlein über Glauben und Taufe . . ." in C. J. Dyck, ed., *A Legacy of Faith*, Newton, 1962, p. 213, see esp. note 67, p. 256); (c) Balthasar Hubmaier's booklet "Von dem christlichen Tauf der Gläubigen" (*On the Christian Baptism of Believers*) written in July, 1525 in Gunnar Westin & Torsten Bergsten et al, ed., *Balthasar Hubmaier: Schriften*, Gütersloh, 1962, pp. 116 ff. Neither of the specific emphases of the Strasbourg letter is of major significance in these earlier sources. This might indicate that they are Sattler's own unique contribution to earliest Anabaptist thought, perhaps partly illuminated by his heritage in the Benedictine order, which was the West's oldest renewal movement. Cf. note 19.

19. Dr. Jean Seguy of Paris has suggested that these emphases are comparable with those of other visions of church reform and of discipleship in the devotional tradition of the Benedictines. Especially can this be said of the image of the two camps in battle array or the "two standards," which is portrayed at a strategic point in the spiritual exercises of Ignatius of Loyola. To test such a hypothesis would demand careful comparison not simply of general concepts but of specific verbal usages within South German Benedictine sources. There is, in any case, about the piety of Michael Sattler no sign of the studied management of the development of religious experience which is typical of the rest of the exercises of Loyola.

20. Krebs-Rott, *op. cit.*, No. 70, pp. 68 ff. The first sentence, serving as address, is written across the back of the letter.

21. The pre-eminence of the New Testament within Scripture is taken for granted.

22. 1 Tim. 1:5.

23. "Das es möge gsin," "that it may be" questions the theological appropriateness of the Reformers' thoroughgoing application of the text from 1 Timothy in such a way as consistently to undercut the various New Testament teachings advocated by Sattler.

24. 1 Tim. 1:15 ff. With the exception of the introductory reference to 1 Timothy 1:5, Sattler does not give the biblical references in his letter. The texts being cited or alluded to are labeled following Rott.

25. Mk. 16:16.

26. Rom. 5:1 ff.

27. Rom. 12:5; 1 Cor. 12:12 ff. The Bossert-Bender biography in *ME* adds "now." None of the significant divergences between the *ME* translation and the present rendering is traceable to ambiguities in the original. They rather reflect errors in Bossert's rendering of the German text in *ML*, IV, p. 32.

28. Eph. 1:22. *ME* translates "believing church."

29. 1 Cor. 12:6 ff. Perhaps "minded" (which *ME* omits) refers as well to the thought of Philippians 2:5. Note below the parallel thought in the Schleitheim brotherly union: p. 35, 40, 41.

30. Rom. 8:29.

31. Mk. 9:12, *ME* has "Christ despises the world."

32. Lk. 10:16; Jn. 15:19.

33. Jn. 18:36.

34. 1 Jn. 2:15 ff.; Jas. 4:4.

35. Mt. 10:22.

36. Eph. 2:2; 6:11, "Children of darkness" is the obvious reversal of "children of light" in Lk. 16:8 and Jn. 12:36.

37. Jn. 8:12; 1 Jn. 1:7.

38. Mt. 18:11; 1 Pet. 5:8.

39. Gal. 5:17.

40. Rom. 8:6 ff.

41. (Literally "armament") Lk. 21:15 f. The term here translated "yielded," *gelassen*, could also be rendered "surrendered," but not "at rest" (so in *ME*). This usage is a most significant testimony to the concept of surrenderedness or *Gelassenheit*, making evident that it has immediately an ethical implication, not only a mystical one.

42. Heb. 10:34; 13:14.

43. Eph. 2:19.

44. Mt. 7:21, Rom. 2:13.

45. Mt. 16:17; 1 Cor. 15:15.

46. 2 Cor. 6:15. Bossert includes point 20 as part of 19.

47. I.e., keeps me from agreeing with. The reference to "Paul" is the same as at the beginning of the text; love is the end of the commandment. For further detail as to how the concept of "love" functioned for the Reformers as an alternative to the direct application of biblical commands, cf. Heinrich Bullinger, "How to Deal with Anabaptists," *MQR*, XXXIII, April 1959, pp. 83 ff. "The rule of faith and love" is for Bullinger quite specifically the alternative to literal interpretation (pp. 90 f., 91 note 27, 95). Cf. further the chapter on the "Rule of Love" in J. Yoder, *Täufertum und Reformation in Gespräch*, Zürich, 1968, pp. 44 ff.

48. "*dem widerwärtigen weichen.*" *Weichen* may mean either "withdraw" or more actively "shun." Sattler probably alluding to Rom. 16:17 or Tit. 3:10. This passage is the evidence that Sattler may well have thought of staying in Strasbourg, since his determination to leave results directly from his inability to reach agreement with Bucer and Capito on the points at issue. This further suggests that if he had stayed, it would have been in some relationship of collaboration or at least mutual respect with these two men. In other words, even though he came to Strasbourg more than a year after the birth of Anabaptism in Zürich, and even after the first expulsion of an Anabaptist by the Strasbourg authorities (Hans Wolff of Benfeld, June 13, 1526), Sattler did not enter the city with the settled sectarian assumption that he belonged to a group which had already taken for granted its being rejected by the authorities. He still approached the Reformers as brothers with whom conversation could continue. Even when Denck was forced out it seems that Sattler contemplated staying.

49. Literally "will finally do it": in the sense of "man proposes, God disposes."

50. The reference here to "those in error" does not distinguish between Anabaptists and state-church Protestants, since that distinction has not yet been frozen. Cf. page 50, note 39. The freedom here advocated by Bucer and Capito (p. 15) is not clearly distinct from that against which the Schleitheim cover letter was directed (pp. 35, 36). Cf. also p. 64, note 19. Capito's view on dealing with those in error was the same as that expressed here (cf. pp. 88 ff.).

51. This is one of the early Anabaptist expressions concerning religious liberty and its relation to church discipline. Cf. Schleitheim Art. II, below, p. 36. See also Art. IV, p. 38.

II

The Schleitheim
Brotherly Union

(February 1527)

Introduction

At the beginning of 1527 the Swiss Brethren movement stood in serious danger of disintegration. The repression from the Protestant side had reached for the first time the level of capital punishment, with the execution of Felix Mantz in Zürich, January 5. In eastern Switzerland, where the movement had met with an initial wave of popular success, it had been put down very firmly in the city of St. Gall but the authorities continued to have difficulty in the surrounding countryside, especially in the canton of Appenzell, where the combination of governmental pressure, inadequate leadership, and the socioeconomic ferment of the times led to a degree of disorder which Conrad Grebel was probably attempting to counteract when he died of illness in the summer of 1526. Strasbourg was the place where the greatest likelihood had remained open that an understanding, or at least the possibility of a continuing conversation, might be reached, between the Anabaptists and the official Reformation; but this possibility had to be abandoned after Sattler's visit in Strasbourg.[1]

Strasbourg should have been the best, and was therefore also the last, chance to break through to serious understanding with leaders of the "mainstream" Reformation movement.

The town of Schleitheim on the Swiss-German border.

The Täuferwegli (Trail of the Anabaptists) leads from Schleitheim to the forest Am Randen, in which the Brethren held meetings in secret.

Martin Bucer was the most ecumenically and pastorally minded of the major Reformers, Capito the most open to radical ideas, the Strasbourg government the most cautious and tolerant. When conversations broke off there, not quite two years after the first break in Zürich, it had become irrevocably clear that Anabaptism would have to go it alone, not only in the territories remaining strictly Roman Catholic, but everywhere.

This marks the end of Sattler's investment in "interchurch relations." He forsook the effort to convince the Reformed leaders; at the same time he forsook the possibility of extending his movement in the Protestant territories where it would have been both easier (due to the undercurrent of sympathies for his concerns) and safer (due to the slightly milder persecution). Henceforth he would work in the smaller towns of the Black Forest. This area was partly directly under Austrian (i.e., faithfully Catholic) sovereignty, partly under the administration of Austria's *Statthalter* of Ensisheim, and elsewhere under Austria's allies and vassals, like Count Joachim von Zollern of Hohenberg, who was to become Sattler's judge.

This stretch of Catholic countryside, with no major cities between Ulm and Freiburg or between Tübingen and Schaffhausen, could be spoken of as the northern growing edge of the Swiss Brethren movement. In the triangle Schaffhausen/Waldshut/Zürich its territory intersected with the southern wing. Sattler and Wilhelm Röubli/Reublin were its only prominent leaders in this earliest period.

Sattler may well have been quite conscious that little time now remained to consolidate the movement he had planted. Just as October-December 1523 marked the first self-awareness of the Zürich radicals and December 1524-January 1525 the first formal breach, so early 1527 must be recognized as the coming-of-age of a distinct, visible fellowship taking long-range responsibility for its order and its faith.

Pressure from the outside, confusion from the inside, loss of the guiding influence (which had never been especially clear or authoritative) of the Zürich founders, and the growing realization that instead of holding forth a vision for widespread renewal the young movement would have to accept a continuing separate, suffering identity, combined to make it quite possible that the entire movement might now filter away into the sand.

It was to this need that the Schleitheim meeting spoke. We know nothing of how the meeting was called, the precise provocation which led it to take place just at this moment, or who participated. The tradition according to which Michael Sattler was the leading spirit in the meeting, and the author of the document reproduced below, is so widespread as to be worthy of belief,[2] even though none of the early traditions to that effect are eyewitness reports. This tradition is confirmed by obvious parallels in thought and phrasing between the Schleitheim text and the other writings known genuinely to be from Sattler's hand.

Oldest existing copy of the "Brotherly Union" of 1527 in the Sammelband, Mennonite Historical Library, Goshen, Indiana.

The *Seven Articles,* which are the heart of the text, were presumably discussed, rewritten, and approved in the course of the meeting. Here Sattler's contribution may well have been some drafting prior to the meeting. The *Seven Articles* are imbedded in a letter written in the first person after the meeting, which is presumably altogether from the pen of Sattler.

Scholars have for some time been divided about the primary focus of this meeting. Jan Kiwiet has stated most strongly the argument that the primary polemic focus was upon the threats from within the Anabaptist movement, represented by the broader minds of men like Hans Denck in Germany, with their criticism of the more rigorous discipline of the Swiss Brethren movement.[3] The strength of this interpretation lies not in the *Seven Articles* themselves, but in the cover letter, and in the spirit of some of the other writings in this collection.[4]

The other interpretation begins with the observation that, differing from a balanced catechism or creed, Schleitheim concentrated upon those points at which the brothers differed from the rest of Protestantism. It was thus a common man's handbook on Anabaptist distinctives. This interpretation is supported by the content of the *Seven Articles* themselves, which often circulated without the cover letter. This is the way this text was understood by the Reformers[5] and it is today supported by Beatrice Jenny.[6]

The present editor sees no real need to choose between the two interpretations. If there were persons vying for leadership within the young Anabaptist movement, the most obvious direction in which they would have led, in conflict to the orientation set by the Zürich beginners and Michael Sattler, would have been toward a spiritualizing of the distinctiveness of the visible Anabaptist congregations, with the effect of greater subservience, at least superficially, to the state church authorities, and greater conformity to the patterns of behavior they required. The later documents in this collection confirm that one of the traits of "false prophets" and "evil overseers" was that they justified attendance at state church gatherings.[7] Even the antinomian "carnal liberty" of those who argued that since one is in Christ one can do anything without harm,[8] may be applied to arguments for conformity to the state church in externals just as appropriately as to drunkenness or disorderly social relations. The idea that if one is a believer one can do anything at all without harm to one's faith was not a peculiar and licentious invention of some marginal Anabaptist; it was (at least according to the misinterpretation of the popular mind) one of the outworkings of Lutheran preaching when distorted by the desires of the listener.[9]

There is thus no reason to need to decide between the two foci referred to above.[10] The clear statement of what distinguishes the Swiss Brethren movement from the Protestant and Catholic churches was at the same time the solidest defense against confusion and cross purposes within the ranks of the brotherhood as it began to take form as an autonomous movement.

The strategic significance of the achievement of Schleitheim is well demonstrated by the rapid and wide circulation of our text. Zwingli received his first copy in April from Johannes Oekolampad, who in turn had received it from Johannes Grell, a country pastor near Basel. Soon he received another copy from Berchtold Haller in Bern. This copy had been seized by the Bern police in the course of a search of homes, following an effort of four Anabaptists to converse with Haller. Haller called it "their aims and grounds." Zwingli responded immediately with a refutation.[11] By the time Zwingli wrote his *Elenchus* in the summer of that year he had in hand four different copies which had come to him from as many different sources. We have surveyed above[12] the number of reprintings and translations which the *Brotherly Union*, together with some of the other following materials, underwent; in these pamphlets it was the Schleitheim text which appeared first and which gave its name to the title page of the entire collection.

According to Zwingli, "There is almost no one among you who does not have a copy of your so well founded commandments."[13] Calvin describes the outline as "seven articles to which all Anabaptists in common adhere . . . which they hold to be a revelation come down from heaven."[14] The authority which came to be ascribed to the *Seven Articles* within the Anabaptist movement is demonstrated on one hand by the nearly universal acceptance of the positions it represents, visible even in the repetition of phrasing and arguments in later documents. Especially is this true with regard to articles VI and VII, on the sword and the oath, and results in a relatively great uniformity in Anabaptist positions on these matters from now on.[15] As late as 1557, we find the importance of the meeting being underlined by reference to the fact that one man at the 1557 Strasbourg conference was the person in whose home the agreement had been drawn up.[16] The text of Schleitheim can also be cited explicitly.[17]

The textual basis of the present translation is that prepared by Dr. Heinold Fast in his edition of the *Täuferakten* for eastern Switzerland, graciously communicated before publication. The effort to establish the original text by critical conjecture must work with four sources: (a) Zwingli's *Elenchus*, within which the full text is translated into Latin on the basis of the four copies Zwingli had in hand. This was the basis for the earliest translation into English.[18] (b) The manuscript preserved in the Berner Staatsarchiv,[19] reproduced once partially by Ernst Mueller, *Geschichte der Bernischen*, Frauenfeld, 1895, Täufer, 38 ff., and more fully but still not with complete accuracy (cf. Fast), by Beatrice Jenny, *Bekenntnis*. There are good reasons to believe that this was one of the four texts Zwingli had before him, but it does not always coincide with his Latin translation and a few times the other reading reflected in his translations seems preferable. (c) The early print reproduced by Böhmer in 1912.[20] (d) The early print reproduced by Köhler in 1908.[21]

The two early prints are very similar. They were the basis for all the later printings, for the translations into French and Dutch, and for the manuscript copies preserved by the Hutterian Brethren and later reprinted by Wolkan,[22] Beck,[23] and Lydia Müller.[24] Köhler's reprint is the basis as well of the widely used English translation by J. C. Wenger.[25]

Since its recognition by the Dutch historian, Cramer, perhaps the first modern witness to the deep significance of Schleitheim, comments on the text and its importance have been frequent.[26] Several summaries of the history of the text are available.[27] Modern translations have been prepared in English[28] and French[29] and Heinold Fast has published a modern German version as well as re-editing the original.[30]

To the *Brotherly Understanding*, which in the past two generations has come to be widely recognized as a theological landmark, we append another text which may well have been equally significant at the time. This set of instructions concerning congregational order and worship was circulating in April 17, 1527, together with the Schleitheim text, apparently in the same hand as the Bern text of the *Brotherly Union.* It therefore must have been seized at the same time in April, within six weeks of the Schleitheim gathering. It therefore has circumstantial grounds for being considered as linked with Schleitheim and with Sattler. It is the oldest known text on its subject, and has not previously been published in full.

The Text

Brotherly Union of a Number of Children of God Concerning Seven Articles

The Cover Letter

May joy, peace, mercy from our Father, through the atonement[31] of the blood of Christ Jesus, together with the gifts of the Spirit — who is sent by the Father to all believers to [give] strength and consolation and constance in all tribulation until the end, Amen, be with all who love God and all children of light, who are scattered everywhere, wherever they might have been placed[32] by God our Father, wherever they might be gathered in unity of spirit in one God and Father of us all; grace and peace of heart be with you all. Amen.

Beloved brothers and sisters in the Lord; first and primordially we are always concerned for your consolation and the assurance of your conscience (which was sometime confused), so that you might not always be separated from us as aliens and by right almost completely excluded,[33] but that you might turn to the true implanted members of Christ, who have been armed through patience and the knowledge of self, and thus be again united with us in the power of a godly Christian spirit and zeal for God.

It is manifest with what manifold cunning the devil has turned us aside, so that he might destroy and cast down the work of God, which in us mercifully and graciously has been partially begun. But the true Shepherd of our souls, Christ, who has begun such in us, will direct and teach[34] the same unto the end, to His glory and our salvation, Amen.

Dear brothers and sisters, we who have been assembled in the Lord at Schleitheim on the Randen[35] make known, in points and articles, unto all that love God, that as far as we are concerned, we have been united[36] to stand fast in the Lord as obedient children of God, sons and daughters, who have been and shall be separated from the world in all that we do and leave undone, and (the praise and glory be to God alone) uncontradicted by all the brothers, completely at peace.[37] Herein we have sensed the unity of the Father and of our common Christ as present with us in their Spirit. For the Lord is a Lord of peace and not of quarreling, as Paul indicates.[38] So that you understand at what points this occurred, you should observe and understand [what follows]:

A very great offense has been introduced by some false brothers among us,[39] whereby several have turned away from the faith, thinking to practice and observe the freedom of the Spirit and of Christ. But such have fallen short of the truth and (to their own condemnation)[40] are given over to the lasciviousness and license of the flesh. They have esteemed that faith and love may do and permit everything and that nothing can harm nor condemn them, since they are "believers."

Note well, you members[41] of God in Christ Jesus, that faith in the heavenly Father through Jesus Christ is not thus formed; it produces and brings forth no such things as these false brothers and sisters practice and teach. Guard yourselves and be warned of such people, for they do not serve our Father, but their father, the devil.

But for you it is not so; for they who are Christ's have crucified their flesh with all its lusts and desires.[42] You understand me[43] well, and [know] the brothers whom we mean. Separate yourselves from them, for they are perverted. Pray the Lord that they may have knowledge unto repentance, and for us that we may have constance to persevere along the path we have entered upon, unto the glory of God and of Christ His Son. Amen.[44]

[The Seven Articles]

The articles we have dealt with, and in which we have been united,[45] are these: baptism, ban, the breaking of bread, separation from abomination, shepherds in the congregation, the sword, the oath.

I. Notice concerning baptism. Baptism shall be given to all those who have been taught repentance and the amendment of life and [who] believe truly that their sins are taken away through Christ, and to all those who desire to walk in the resurrection of Jesus Christ and be buried with Him in death, so that they might rise with Him; to all those who with such an understanding themselves desire and request it from us; hereby is excluded all infant baptism, the greatest and first abomination of the Pope. For this you have the reasons and the testimony of the writings and the practice of the apostles.[46] We wish simply yet resolutely and with assurance to hold to the same.

II. We have been united as follows concerning the ban.

The ban shall be employed with all those who have given themselves over to the Lord, to walk after [Him][47] in His commandments; those who have been baptized into the one body of Christ, and let themselves be called brothers or sisters, and still somehow slip and fall into error and sin, being inadvertently overtaken.[48] The same [shall] be warned twice privately and the third time be publicly admonished before the entire congregation[49] according to the command of Christ (Mt. 18).[50] But this shall be done according to the ordering of the Spirit of God before the breaking of bread,[51] so that we may all in one spirit and in one love break and eat from one bread and drink from one cup.

III. Concerning the breaking of bread, we have become one and agree[52] thus: all those who desire to break the one bread in remembrance of the broken body of Christ and all those who wish to drink of one drink in remembrance of the shed blood of Christ, they must beforehand be united[53] in the one body of Christ, that is the congregation of God, whose head is Christ, and that by baptism. For as Paul indicates,[54] we cannot be partakers at the same time of the table of the Lord and the table of devils. Nor can we at the same time partake and drink of the cup of the Lord and the cup of devils. That is: all those who have fellowship with the dead works of darkness have no part in the light. Thus all who follow the devil and the world, have no part with those who have been called out of the world unto God. All those who lie in evil have no part in the good.

So it shall and must be, that whoever does not share the calling of the one God to one faith, to one baptism, to one spirit, to one body together with all the children of God, may not be made one loaf together with them, as must be true if one wishes truly to break bread according to the command of Christ.[55]

IV. We have been united concerning the separation that shall take place from the evil and the wickedness which the devil has planted in the world, simply in this; that we have no fellowship with them,[56] and do not run with them in the confusion of their abominations. So it is; since all who have not entered into the obedience of faith and have not united themselves with God so that they will to do His will, are a great abomination before God, therefore nothing else can or really will grow or spring forth from them than abominable things. Now there is nothing else in the world and all creation than good or evil, believing and unbelieving, darkness and light, the world and those who are [come] out of the world, God's temple and idols, Christ and Belial, and none will have part with the other.

To us, then, the commandment of the Lord is also obvious, whereby He orders us to be and to become separated from the evil one, and thus He will be our God and we shall be His sons and daughters.[57]

Further, He admonishes us therefore to go out from Babylon and from the earthly Egypt, that we may not be partakers in their torment and suffering, which the Lord will bring upon them.[58]

From all this we should learn that everything which has not been united[59] with our God in Christ is nothing but an abomination which we should shun.[60] By this are meant all popish and repopish[61] works and idolatry,[62] gatherings, church attendance,[63] winehouses, guarantees and commitments of unbelief,[64] and other things of the kind, which the world regards highly, and yet which are carnal or flatly counter to the command of God, after the pattern of all the iniquity which is in the world. From all this we shall be separated and have no part with such, for they are nothing but abominations, which cause us to be hated before our Christ Jesus, who has freed us from the servitude of the flesh and fitted us for the service of God and the Spirit whom He has given us.

Thereby shall also[65] fall away from us the[66] diabolical weapons of violence — such as sword, armor, and the like, and all of their use to protect friends or against enemies —by virtue of the word of Christ: "you shall not resist evil."[67]

V. We have been united as follows concerning shepherds in the church of God. The shepherd in the church shall be a person according to the rule of Paul,[68] fully and completely, who has a good report of those who are outside the faith. The office of such a person shall be to read and exhort and teach, warn, admonish, or ban in the congregation, and properly to preside among the sisters and brothers in prayer, and in the breaking of bread,[69] and in all things to take care of the body of Christ, that it may be built up and developed, so that the name of God might be praised and honored through us, and the mouth of the mocker be stopped.

He shall be supported, wherein he has need, by the congregation which has chosen him, so that he who serves the gospel can also live therefrom, as the Lord has ordered.[70] But should a shepherd do something worthy of reprimand, nothing shall be done with him without the voice of two or three witnesses. If they sin they shall be publicly reprimanded, so that others might fear.[71]

But if the shepherd should be driven away or led to the Lord by the cross,[72] at the same hour another shall be ordained[73] to his place, so that the little folk and the little flock of God may not be destroyed, but be preserved by warning and be consoled.

VI. We have been united as follows concerning the sword. The sword is an ordering of God outside the perfection of Christ. It punishes and kills the wicked, and guards and protects the good. In the law the sword is established[74] over the wicked for punishment and for death, and the secular rulers are established to wield the same.

But within the perfection of Christ only the ban is used for the admonition and exclusion of the one who has sinned, without the death of the flesh,[75] simply the warning and the command to sin no more.

Now many, who do not understand Christ's will for us, will ask: whether a Christian may or should use the sword against the wicked for the protection and defense of the good, or for the sake of love.

The answer is unanimously revealed: Christ teaches and

commands us to learn from Him, for He is meek and lowly of heart and thus we shall find rest for our souls.[76] Now Christ says to the woman who was taken in adultery,[77] not that she should be stoned according to the law of His Father (and yet He says, "what the Father commanded me, that I do")[78] but with mercy and forgiveness and the warning to sin no more, says: "Go, sin no more." Exactly thus should we also proceed, according to the rule of the ban.

Second, is asked concerning the sword: whether a Christian shall pass sentence in disputes and strife about worldly matters, such as the unbelievers have with one another. The answer: Christ did not wish to decide or pass judgment between brother and brother concerning inheritance, but refused to do so.[79] So should we also do.

Third, is asked concerning the sword: whether the Christian should be a magistrate if he is chosen thereto. This is answered thus: Christ was to be made king, but He fled and did not discern the ordinance of His Father.[80] Thus we should also do as He did and follow after Him, and we shall not walk in darkness. For He Himself says: "Whoever would come after me, let him deny himself and take up his cross and follow me.[81] He Himself further forbids the violence of the sword when He says; "The princes of this world lord it over them etc., but among you it shall not be so."[82] Further Paul says, "Whom God has foreknown, the same he has also predestined to be conformed to the image of his Son," etc.[83] Peter also says: "Christ has suffered (not ruled) and has left us an example, that you should follow after in his steps."[84]

Lastly one can see in the following points that it does not befit a Christian to be a magistrate: the rule of the government is according to the flesh, that of the Christians according to the spirit. Their houses and dwelling remain in this world, that of the Christians is in heaven. Their citizenship is in this world, that of the Christians is in heaven.[85] The weapons of their battle and warfare are carnal and only against the flesh, but the weapons of Christians are spiritual, against the fortification of the devil. The worldly are armed with steel and iron, but Christians are armed with the armor of God, with truth, righteousness, peace, faith, salvation, and with the Word of God. In sum: as Christ our Head is minded, so also must be minded the members of the body of Christ through Him, so that there be no division in the body, through which it would be destroyed.[86] Since then Christ is as is written of Him, so must His members also be the same, so that His body may remain whole and unified for its own advancement and upbuilding. For any kingdom which is divided within itself will be destroyed.[87]

VII. We have been united as follows concerning the oath. The oath is a confirmation among those who are quarreling or making promises. In the law it is commanded that it should be done only in the name of God, truthfully and not falsely. Christ, who teaches the perfection of the law, forbids His [followers] all swearing, whether true nor false; neither by heaven nor by earth, neither by Jerusalem nor by our head; and that for the reason which He goes on to give: "For you cannot make one hair white or black." You see, thereby all swearing is forbidden. We cannot perform what is promised in swearing, for we are not able to change the smallest part of ourselves.[88]

Now there are some who do not believe the simple commandment of God and who say, "But God swore by Himself to Abraham, because He was God (as He promised him that He would do good to him and would be his God if he kept His commandments). Why then should I not swear if I promise something to someone?" The answer: hear what Scripture says: "God, since he wished to prove overabundantly to the heirs of His promise that His will did not change, inserted an oath so that by two immutable things we might have a stronger consolation (for it is impossible that God should lie)".[89] Notice the meaning of the passage: God has the power to do what He forbids you, for everything is possible to Him. God swore an oath to Abraham, Scripture says, in order to prove that His counsel is immutable. That means: no one can withstand and thwart His will; thus He can keep His oath. But we cannot, as Christ said above, hold or perform our oath, therefore we should not swear.

Others say that swearing cannot be forbidden by God in the New Testament when it was commanded in the Old, but that it is forbidden only to swear by heaven, earth, Jerusalem, and our head. Answer: hear the Scripture. He who swears by heaven, swears by God's throne and by Him who sits thereon.[90] Observe: swearing by heaven is forbidden, which is only God's throne; how much more is it forbidden to swear by God Himself. You blind fools, what is greater, the throne or He who sits upon it?

Others say, if it is then wrong to use God for truth, then the apostles Peter and Paul also swore.[91] Answer: Peter and Paul only testify to that which God promised Abraham, whom we long after have received. But when one testifies, one testifies concerning that which is present, whether it be good or evil. Thus Simeon spoke of Christ to Mary and testified: "Behold: this one is ordained for the falling and rising of many in Israel and to be a sign which will be spoken against."[92]

Christ taught us similarly when He says:[93] Your speech shall be yea, yea; and nay, nay; for what is more than that comes of evil. He says, your speech or your word shall be yes and no, so that no one might understand that He had permitted it. Christ is simply yea and nay, and all those who seek Him simply will understand His Word. Amen.[94]

The Cover Letter

Dear Brothers and Sisters in the Lord; these are the articles which some brothers previously had understood wrongly and in a way not conformed to the true meaning. Thereby many weak consciences were confused, whereby the name of God has been grossly slandered, for which reason it was needful that we should be brought to agreement[95] in the Lord, which has come to pass. To God be praise and glory!

Now that you have abundantly understood the will of God as revealed through us at this time, you must fulfill this will, now known, persistently and unswervingly. For you know well what is the reward of the servant who knowingly sins.

Everything which you have done unknowingly and now confess to have done wrongly, is forgiven you, through that believing prayer, which is offered among us in our meeting for all our shortcomings and guilt, through the gracious forgiveness of God and through the blood of Jesus Christ. Amen.

Watch out for all who do not walk in simplicity of divine truth, which has been stated by us in this letter in our meeting, so that everyone might be governed among us by the rule of the ban, and that henceforth the entry of false brothers and sisters among us might be prevented.

Put away from you that which is evil, and the Lord will be your God, and you will be His sons and daughters.[96]

Dear brothers, keep in mind what Paul admonished Titus.[97] He says: "The saving grace of God has appeared to all, and disciplines us, that we should deny ungodliness and worldly lusts, and live circumspect righteous and godly lives in this world; awaiting the same hope and the appearing of the glory of the great God and of our Savior Jesus Christ, who gave himself for us, to redeem us from all unrighteousness and to purify unto himself a people of his own, that would be zealous of good works." Think on this, and exercise yourselves therein, and the Lord of peace will be with you.

May the name of God be forever blessed and greatly praised, Amen. May the Lord give you His peace, Amen.

Done at Schleitheim, St. Matthew's Day,[98] Anno MDXXVII.

Congregational Order[99]

Since the almighty eternal and merciful God has made His wonderful light break forth in this world and [in this] most dangerous time, we recognize the mystery of the divine will, that the Word is preached to us according to the proper ordering of the Lord,[100] whereby we have been called into His fellowship. Therefore, according to the command of the Lord and the teachings of His apostles, in Christian order, we should observe the new commandment[101] in love one toward another, so that love and unity may be maintained, which all brothers and sisters of the entire congregation should agree to hold to as follows:

1. The brothers and sisters should meet at least three or four times a week, to exercise themselves[102] in the teaching of Christ and His apostles and heartily to exhort one another to remain faithful to the Lord as they have pledged.

2. When the brothers and sisters are together, they shall take up something to read together.[103] The one to whom God has given the best understanding shall explain it,[104] the others should be still and listen, so that there are not two or three carrying on a private conversation, bothering the others. The Psalter shall be read daily at home.[105]

3. Let none be frivolous in the church of God, neither in words nor in actions. Good conduct shall be maintained by them all also before the heathen.[106]

4. When a brother sees his brother erring, he shall warn him according to the command of Christ,[107] and shall admonish him in a Christian and brotherly way, as everyone is bound and obliged to do out of love.

5. Of all the brothers and sisters of this congregation none shall have anything of his own, but rather, as the Christians in the time of the apostles held all in common, and especially stored up a common fund, from which aid can be given to the poor, according as each will have need,[108] and as in the apostles' time permit no brother to be in need.

6. All gluttony shall be avoided among the brothers who are gathered in the congregation; serve a soup or a minimum of vegetable and meat, for eating and drinking are not the kingdom of heaven.[109]

7. The Lord's Supper shall be held, as often as the brothers are together,[110] thereby proclaiming the death of the Lord, and thereby warning each one to commemorate, how Christ gave His life for us, and shed His blood for us, that we might also be willing to give our body and life for Christ's sake, which means for the sake of all the brothers.

Notes

1. See above item I, Goeters, *op. cit.*, p. 94, supports the hypothesis that when at Strasbourg Sattler still had some hope of working in unity with Bucer and Capito, i.e., of winning them and their Reformation as a whole for movement in the direction of Anabaptism. Goeters underlines that the Strasbourg twenty articles differ from the Schleitheim seven articles chiefly in that Strasbourg recognizes no necessity for a pastoral office, while Schleitheim does. This suggests that the final abandonment of the vision of successful conversation with the Reformers did not come until early 1527.

2. The earliest explicit testimony to this tradition is in a tract of Leopold Scharnschlager which quotes article VI regarding government (*ARG*, 1956, p. 212). See also H. Strieker, *MGB*, 21, 1964, p. 15.

3. Jan Kiwiet, *Pilgram Marpeck*, Kassel, 1957, pp. 43 ff.; cf. also George Huntston Williams, *The Radical Reformation*, Philadelphia, 1962, p. 182; cf. below p. 48, note 33.

4. See below pp. 126 ff.

5. "They included the sum of what they hold which is contrary both to us and to the papists, in seven articles . . ." Calvin, *Brieve Instruction, op. cit.*, p. 44.

Thus it was most appropriate that Calvin should take this text as the outline of his own refutation. Zwingli likewise considered the *Seven Articles* a most appropriate outline for a refutation; immediately upon receiving the first manuscript from Berchtold Haller of Bern he responded at length with a letter, answering point by point, on April 28, 1527 (Z, vol. IX, letter No. 610, p. 108); again the use of the *Seven Articles* in Zwingli's *Elenchus* is a testimony to their representative character. It cannot be the concern of this volume to review at length these refutations by the Reformers or the substantial differences between them; we shall refer to the Zwingli and Calvin texts only as they assist us in textual criticism.

6. Beatrice Jenny, *Das Schleitheimer Täuferbekenntnis*, Thayngen, 1951, p. 39.

7. See below especially pp. 60, 127 ff.

8. This thrust of the position against which the *Brotherly Union* is directed is evident especially in the introductory paragraphs of Michael Sattler's cover letter. Reference to a similar concern can be seen as well in the later tracts (below pp. 108 ff). 149, 170, 172).

9. Zwingli points to the same danger in his tract of December 1524, "Wer Ursache gibt zu Aufruhr" (Z, III, pp. 374 ff). A major source of social unrest, Zwingli says, is those persons who misinterpret gospel preaching as a loosening of sound moral requirements. This topic was later to become one of the standing disagreements between the Anabaptists and the official Protestantism (cf. Harold Bender, "Walking in the Resurrection," *MQR*, XXXV, April 1961, pp. 96 ff.). The popularity of contextual ethics in American Protestantism in the late 1960s is further testimony that such a position is quite thinkable in Protestant circles.

10. Cf. below note 39 a further reference to this theme.

11. Cf. note 5 above.

12. Note above survey of printing, 13 f.

13. Z, VI, p. 106. His major treatise, *Contra Catabaptistarum Strophas Elenchus*, "Refutation of the Catabaptists' Knaveries" (1527) was Zwingli's final settlement with the Anabaptist issue, his only Latin writing on the subject. In addition to the *Seven Articles* it also refutes a "confutation booklet," written perhaps by Conrad Grebel and directed specifically against Zwingli himself (Yoder, *Gespräche*, pp. 91 ff.). The *Elenchus* is available in English translation; see below note 28.

The term *catabaptist* used here predominantly by Zwingli was borrowed from Oekolampad, but did not establish itself, being replaced progressively by *anabaptist*. The German prefix *wider-* can mean either "counter-" or "re-"; thus the appellation *widertouff* can bear three or four possible meanings: (a) anti-baptism in the sense of being practiced in opposition to the traditional infant baptism; (b) anti-baptism in the sense of being a perversion or a parody of the true sacrament; (c) re-baptism; (d) it might even mean "immersers" (*kata-* also means "down" or "under.") This would seem to have been Oekolampad's understanding. Zwingli's usage of *kata-* is intended to preserve the force of the German polyvalence of meaning, with the accent on the sense of perversion (b above). Cf. Fritz Blanke's extensive explanatory note, Z, VI, p. 21, note 1.

14. *CR*, XXXV, p. 54.

15. James M. Stayer, whose work on this theme, "The Doctrine of the Sword in the First Decade of Anabaptism," Cornell PhD dissertation 1964, gives the most attention to chronological development, divides the entire treatment into the periods "before and after the impact of Schleitheim."

Clarence Bauman, *Gewaltlosigkeit im Täufertum*, Leiden, 1968, calls Schleitheim "the most important document for the time of the founding of Anabaptism" (p. 45).

Hans J. Hillerbrand, *Die Politische Ethik des Oberdeutschen Täufertums*, Leiden/Köln 1962, and "The Anabaptist View of the State" (*MQR*, XXXII, April 1958, pp. 83 ff.), disregards the aspect of chronological development and therefore gives more attention to later and longer texts.

16. Blaupot ten Cate, *Geschiedenis der Doopsgezinden in Groningen*, emz. 1842, I, pp. 258 ff., and Hulshof, *Geschiedenis van de Doopsgezinden te Straatsburg van 1525 tot 1557*, Amsterdam, 1905, p. 229. This is a part of a letter reporting on the major Anabaptist conference in Strasbourg in 1557, one of the major landmarks in relation between South German Anabaptists and the Mennonites of the Netherlands. The letter was translated into Dutch before 1587, and has been preserved only in that version.

17. Cf. above note 2.

18. Z, VI, pp. 107-155. Translation see below, note 28.
19. UP 80.
20. The print identified above 13 as A.
21. The print identified above 13 as B.
22. Rudolf Wolkan, *Geschichtsbuch der Hutterischen Brüder*, Vienna, 1918, p. 42.
23. Josef Beck, *Die Geschichtsbücher der Wiedertäufer...*, Vienna, 1883, pp. 41 ff.
24. Lydia Müller, *Glaubenszeugnisse Oberdeutscher Taufgesinnten*, Leipzig, 1938, p. 37.
25. First printed in *MQR*, XIX, No. 4, October 1945, pp. 247 ff., and then in Wenger's *Doctrines of the Mennonites*, Scottdale, 1952; reproduced from Wenger by Harry Emerson Fosdick: *Great Voices of the Reformation*, New York, 1952; John H. Leith, *Creeds of the Churches*, Garden City, 1963; and Robert L. Ferm, *Readings in the History of Christian Thought*, New York, 1964, pp. 528 ff.
26. "In this so brief, so clear, so easily retained way they rendered a service to the Anabaptists of their day and later, for which they cannot be grateful enough. Certainly they did what they did in all simplicity of heart, and with no ideas of world conquest. They were driven by no other goal than to be responsible for their church, according to God's will for her. They had really nothing at all to do with high ideals; they rather set rules, prescriptions and proscriptions, by means of which the church in the present can guide her doing and her leaving undone. Thereby they performed a good work in the interest of a future of which they themselves could hardly think. They thus brought firmness and definiteness into the spiritual movement in which they had been placed. They saved it from the danger of becoming a chaos of unstable, confused, and confusing ideas, of floating groups, fostered by the most varied tendencies, mostly contradictory, even though [they were] mostly (not always) well-meaning people. Through their formulation they drew the boundaries of their movement and made it possible that an ordered fellowship, an organization, modest as it was, came into being. By creating such solid forms for the unique Christianity of their brotherhood, Sattler and his fellow elders preserved it from diffusion, helped it through the somber days of bloody persecution, and assured it a future. Not a single trait of the 'Brotherly Union' do we fail to find again in the later Mennonite brotherhood. Hardly a phrase does not recur." Cramer, *BRN*, V. 1909, p. 593. Cramer's first statement of the significance of Schleitheim is found in his article *Mennoniten* in *RPTK* Vol. XII, p. 600.
  Our own estimation of the significance of the meeting was first stated independently of Cramer in *Gespräche*, pp. 98 f.: "That it could happen, that in the course of a meeting men could change their opinions and come to unity, is not only a striking rarity in the history of the Reformation; it is also the most important event in the whole history of Anabaptism. Had it not happened, the Anabaptism of Grebel, Blaurock, Mantz, and Sattler would have died out together with its founders. But now it has taken on a viable form and was in a position to resist the licentiousness of the fanatics, the coercion of Christian governments and the persuasiveness of the preachers."
  A very similar judgment is made by W. Köhler: "Not the least important significance of the Schleitheim articles was the creation of an order for the small communities, which in their combat against the established church could so easily disintegrate into anarchy and fanaticism." *Flugschriften*, p. 285. At the occasion of the 1957 unveiling of a memorial to Sattler in the village church at Rottenburg, N. van der Zijpp, then dean of European Mennonite historians, spoke: "Sattler, like Menno Simons, was no founder but rather an organizer of the Anabaptists. For both of them it was necessary to lead a spiritual movement, lively, fervent, prophetic, effervescent, into the path of an organized church. For a spiritual movement like that in Zürich in the years 1525-1526 cannot always remain 'movement,' unless it is ready to abandon itself to the danger of ending in the great sea of fanaticism. Sattler knew quite clearly: the move-

ment had to have form, and he struggled for a form which would at the same time set boundaries and yet preserve freedom. He chose as his slogan 'the fence of Holy Scripture,' just as Menno Simons later emphasized the value of the letter of Holy Scripture. That, perhaps, contains also a danger. But where is the gospel of Jesus Christ perfectly safe among us earthly men?

"The deed of Sattler, like the later one of Menno Simons, set the Anabaptist movement on a solid rock, yea, it saved the church." (*Das Evangelium von Jesus Christus in der Welt: Vorträge und Verhandlungen der Sechsten Mennonitischen Weltkonferenz*, Karlsruhe, 1958, p. 340).

27. Friedmann, *op cit.*, "The Schleitheim Confession . . ." p. 82 ff. Wenger, *op cit.*, "The Schleitheim Confession of Faith" p. 243 ff. Fritz Blanke, "Beobachtungen zum Ältesten Täuferbekenntnis," *ARG*, XXXVII, 1940, pp. 242 ff. *ME*, Vol. I, p. 447. Heinrich Böhmer, *Urkunden zur Geschichte des Bauernkrieges und der Wiedertäufer*, De Gruyter, Berlin, 1933, pp. 25 ff.

28. Samuel Macauley Jackson, who translated Zwingli's *Elenchus* in his *Selected Works of Huldreich Zwingli* (Philadelphia and New York, 1901) pp. 123-258, thereby also translated the *Seven Articles* into English at secondhand. Jackson was ignorant of the existence of the German original and of the document's historical importance. He referred to the text only as "the confession of the Bernese Baptists." This was probably the first English translation of the text, since Calvin's "A Short Instruction . . ." published in London in 1549, included only snatches from the Schleitheim text.

W. J. McGlothlin, who was more aware than Jackson of the significance of the German original, but was still unaware of the existence of several printings in the sixteenth century, reproduced the "Bernese Baptist" translation as Jackson had lifted it from the *Elenchus*, in his *Baptist Confessions of Faith*, Philadelphia, 1911, pp. 3 ff., from where it was taken by Wm. Lumpkin, *Baptist Confessions*, 1959, 22 ff.

The translation by Wenger (see above note 25), which did the most to make American scholars aware of the significance of Schleitheim, is the only modern one before the present re-edition.

29. Pierre Widmer and John Yoder, *"Principes et Doctrines Mennonites,"* Brussels and Montbeliard, 1955, pp. 49-55.

30. Heinold Fast, *Der linke Flügel der Reformation;* Klassiker des Protestantismus, Band IV; Sammlung Dietrich, Bremen, 1962, pp. 60 ff. Fast has also prepared the definitive edition of the original text, which has just appeared in: H. Fast, editor, Band II (Ost-Schweiz) of *Quellen zur Geschichte der Täufer in der Schweiz*, Theologischer Verlag Zürich, 1974, Nr. 26.

31. A most significant concept in the thought of Michael Sattler is that of *Vereinigung*, which, according to the context, must be translated in many different ways. In the title we render it "Union"; here in the salutation it can most naturally be translated "reconciliation" or "atonement"; later in the text, in the passive participle form, it will mean "to be brought to unity." Thus the same word can be used for the reconciling work of Jesus Christ, for the procedure whereby brothers come to a common mind, for the state of agreement in which they find themselves, and for the document which states the agreement to which they have come. Fast suggests that here, in connection with "the blood of Christ," the meaning might be "fellowship"; cf: 1 Cor. 10:16.

32. Or, literally, "ordered"; the rendering of J. C. Wenger, "scattered everywhere as it has been ordained of God our Father," is a good paraphrase if "ordained" may be understood without sacramental or predestinarian connotations.

33. This term "aliens" or "foreigners" was interpreted by Cramer *BRN*, 605, note 1, in a geographic or political sense, as referring to non-Swiss. Kiwiet, *op. cit.*, p. 44, takes for granted the same meaning and says more sharply that the Swiss Anabaptists broke communion with the German ones. This understanding is impossible for several

reasons:
There was no such strong sense of national identity, divided on clear geographic lines, in the 1520s;

Sattler and Reublin, leaders in the meeting, were not Swiss;

The libertines whom Schleitheim had in mind, although Denck (or Bucer) might have been included, were (if Anabaptist) surely mostly Swiss; namely, the enthusiasts of St. Gall (H. Fast "Die Sonderstellung der Täufer in St. Gallen and Appenzell, "*Zwingliana* XI, 1960, pp. 223 ff.), and Ludwig Hätzer.

This term has a quite different reference; it is an allusion to Eph. 2:12 and 19, testifying to the reconciling effect of the gospel on men who previously had been alienated by unbelief.

34. "Direct" and "teach" have as their object "the same," i.e., the "work of God partially begun in us." Wenger's paraphrase, "direct the same and teach [us]" is smoother but weakens the striking image of a "work of God" within man which can be "partially begun," "cast down," "directed," and "taught." There is, however, ground for Böhmer's conjecture that the original may have read *keren* (guide) rather than *leren* (teach).

35. The "Langer Randen" and the "Hoher Randen" are hills overlooking Schleitheim and not, as a modern reader might think, a reference to the fact that Schleitheim is near the (contemporary, political) border.

The original reads "Schlaten am Randen." A good half-dozen villages in southern Germany bear the names Schlat, Schlatt, or Schlatten. One, near Engen in Baden, also is identified as "am Randen," and until recently was held by some to have been the place of origin of the *Seven Articles*. The evidence, now generally accepted, for Schleitheim near Schaffhausen, is easily surveyed:

J. J. Rüger, a Schaffhausen chronicler, writing around 1594, identifies Schleitheim with the *Seven Articles;*

In the local dialect, the equivalent of *ei* in modern German is long *a* as in Schlaten, whereas the other villages Schlatten or Schlat have a short *a*;

Being subject to overlapping jurisdictions and therefore hard to police, the Klettgau, and Schleitheim on its edge, were relatively safe and accessible for Anabaptists and thus a most fitting meeting place linking the major centers in southwest Germany and northeast Switzerland. This was the first area where Sattler's colleague W. Reublin had been active after his expulsion from Zürich early in 1525. This juridical situation continued through the century; Anabaptism was still alive in the Kühtal above Schleitheim as late as Rüger's writing.

Prof. F. Blanke reviews the question of place in Z, VI, pp. 104 f.; cf. also Werner Pletscher, "Wo Entstand das Bekenntnis von 1527?" *MGB*, V, 1940, pp. 20 f.

36. According to Böhmer, one line of print was misplaced in imprint A. The text seems to say literally, "we were assembled in points and articles." The verb here is again "*vereinigt*." The "points and articles" may well have stood elsewhere in the sentence in the original text: "we have been united in points and articles" or "to stand fast in the Lord in these points and articles." Wenger's translation, "we are of one mind to abide in the Lord" is the best paraphrase but sacrifices the passive verbal construction which is important to the writer.

37. Beginning with the parenthesis "(the praise and glory be to God alone)," the closing phrases of this paragraph refer not simply to a common determination to be faithful to the Lord, but much more specifically to the actual Schleitheim experience and the sense of unity (*Vereinigung*) which the members had come to in the course of the meeting. "Without contradiction of all the brothers" is the formal description and "completely at peace" is the subjective definition of this sense of Holy Spirit guidance. Zwingli considered the very report that "we have come together" to be the proof of the culpable, sectarian, conspiratorial character of Anabaptism (*Elenchus, Z, VI, p. 56*).

38. 1 Cor. 14:33.

39. Ds. H. W. Meihuizen has recently asked with great thoroughness "Who were the 'False Brethren' mentioned in the Schleitheim Articles?" *(op. cit.,* pp. 200 ff.). Meihuizen's method is to survey the entire Reformation scene, Anabaptists of all shadings as well as Reformers, especially those at Strasbourg whom Sattler had recently left. Comparing the known theological positions of these men with the Schleitheim statements, Meihuizen concludes that Schleitheim must have been aimed against Denck, Hubmaier, Hut, Hätzer, Bucer, and Capito. One can agree with this description of the positions in question, without being convinced that the meeting was this clearly directed against a few particular men who were specifically not invited. If any one person was meant, it would most likely be Hätzer, whom Sattler had just been with in Strasbourg, and who was the only one of these who could be accused of libertinistic leanings. For present purposes, i.e., in order to understand the meaning of this document, it suffices to be clear from the internal evidence (in agreement with Meihuizen):

That some persons previously attached to some of the positions condemned were present at Schleitheim in order to be participants in the event of "being brought to unity"; the "false brothers" referred to by the cover letter were therefore not only state-church Reformers but at least some of them were within Anabaptism;

That the greatest emphasis in the *Seven Articles* themselves falls on those points of ultimate theological separateness from the Reformed: baptism, relation between ban and the supper, sword, oath. Here the list is so parallel to the document from Strasbourg that one surmises that Sattler may have been developing his outline already when he was at Strasbourg;

That in the juxtaposition of the cover letter and the *Seven Articles,* Sattler affirms an inner linkage between the positions of the marginal Anabaptists and Spiritualists who differed from the Zürich-Schleitheim stream, and those of the evangelical Reformers.

40. H. W. Meihuizen reads the phrase "to their own condemnation" as meaning that the Schleitheim assembly took action to excommunicate the libertines whom the text here refers to. "The Concept of Restitution in the Anabaptism of Northwestern Europe," *MQR,* Vol. XLIV, April 1970, p. 149. This is not possible. The verb *ergeben* refers to the libertines' abandoning themselves to lasciviousness, not to the Anabaptists' action. In order to enable this interpretation Meihuizen must omit the parentheses which are in the original.

41. "Glieder" (members) has in German only the meaning related to the image of the body; the overtone of "membership" in a *group,* which makes the phrase "members of God" unusual in modern English, is not present in the original.

42. Gal. 5:24.

43. The use of the first person singular here is the demonstration that the introductory letter was written, probably after the meeting, by an individual.

44. This is the conclusion of the introductory letter and of the epistolary style. The "cover letter" is not in the Bern manuscript, and the *Seven Articles* probably circulated most often without it.

45. With one exception, every article begins with the same use of the word *vereinigt* as a passive participle, which we have rendered thus literally as a reminder of the meaning of *Vereinigung* for Sattler.

46. Here the printed version identifies the following Scripture texts (giving chapter number only): Mt. 28:19; Mk. 16:6; Acts 2:38; Acts 8:36; Acts 16:31-33; 19:4.

47. *Nachwandeln,* to walk after, is the nearest approximation in the Schleitheim text to the concept of discipleship (*Nachfolge*) which was later to become especially current among Anabaptists.

48. Two interpretations of this phrase are possible. "To be inadvertently over-

taken" might be a description of falling into sin, parallel to the earlier phrase "somehow slip and fall." This would mean that sin is for the Christian disciple partly a matter of ignorance or inattention. Cramer, *BRN*, p. 607, note 2, and Jenny, p. 55, seek to explain that all sin is somehow inadvertent; i.e., that at the time of a sinful decision one is deceived and not fully aware of its gravity. Calvin (with some grounds in the phrasing of the French translation) misunderstood this text to mean that the Anabaptists would distinguish between forgivable and unforgivable sins, with only the inadvertent ones being within the scope of the congregation's reconciling concern. Or the reference may be to the way the guilty person was discovered.

49. The printed version inserts "or banned."

50. This reference to Mt. 18 is the only Scripture reference in the earliest handwritten text. "Rule of Christ" or "Command of Christ" is a standard designation for this text. Cf. J. Yoder: "Binding and Loosing," *Concern 14*, Scottdale, 1967, esp. pp. 15 ff. Other Scripture allusions identified in the footnotes are not labeled in the text. This abundant citation of scriptural language without being concerend to indicate the source of quotation is an indication of the fluency with which Anabaptists thought in biblical vocabulary; it is probably also an indication that they thought of those texts as expressing a meaningful truth rather than as "proof texts."

51. At this point Walter Köhler, the editor of the printed version, suggests the text Mt. 5:23. If "the ordering of the spirit" relates specifically to "before the breaking of bread" and means to point to a Scripture text, this could be a likely one; or 1 Cor. 11 could also possibly be alluded to; but "ordering of the spirit" is not the usual way in which the Anabaptists refer to a Bible quotation. The phrase can also mean a call for a personal and flexible attitude, guided by the Holy Spirit, in the application of the concern for reconciliation.

52. This is the one point at which the word *vereinigt* is not used at the beginning of an article, presumably because it occurs later in the same sentence.

53. *Vereinigt:* here the word has none of the meanings detailed above, but points to still another; to the work of God in constituting the unity of the Christian Church.

54. 1 Cor. 10:21. Some texts have here "*Saint* Paul."

55. Most ecumenical debate about the validity of sacraments focuses upon either the sacramental status of the officiant or the doctrinal understanding of the meaning of the emblems. It should be pointed out that the Anabaptist understanding of close communion refers not to the sacrament but to the participants. It is invalidated not by an unauthorized officiant or an insufficient concept of sacrament, but by the absence of real community among those present.

56. Note the shift from "world" to "they." "The world" is not discussed independently of the people constituting the unregenerate order.

57. 2 Cor. 6:17.

58. Rev. 18:4 ff. Some texts read "which the Lord intends to bring upon them."

59. *Vereinigt.*

60. The printed version adds "and flee."

61. The prefix *wider* can mean either "counter" or "re-" (modern *wieder-*). Both meanings of course apply to the Reformation churches of Strasbourg and the Swiss cities, which are meant here; they are both anti-popish (having broken with the Roman communion) and re-popish (having retained or reinstated certain characteristics of Catholicism). Earlier translations have chosen the rendering "papist and anti-papist," but the other reading carries a greater pointedness of meaning, and is supported by Zwingli's translation. Thus the claim that the new Protestant churches are at some points copies of what was wrong with Catholicism is already taken for granted in early 1527.

62. *Götzendienst.* The Bern manuscript and the early prints read *Gottesdienst* ("worship"); but Zwingli, who had other manuscripts as well, translated "idolatry." Since

the next two words both deal with church attendance, "idolatry" is less redundant. "Idolatry" was a current designation in the whole Zwinglian movement for the place of statues and pictures in Catholic worship.

63. *Kilchgang*, literally meaning church attendance, has no congregational dimension to it but refers to the conformity to established patterns of those who, while perhaps sympathizing with the Anabaptists, still avoided any public reproach by regularly being seen at the state church functions.

64. The Bern manuscript reads *Burgschaft*, i.e., a guarantee or security supporting a promise, and belongs in the economic and social realm. If "unbelief" here refers to a lack of sincerity, then the "guarantees and commitments of unbelief" would mean such matters as signing notes and mortgages and affidavits in less than good faith. Martin Luther held strongly that such guarantees, even in good faith, were not only unwise but immoral since the guarantor puts himself in the place of God. ("On Trading and Usury, 1524," in *Works of Martin Luther*, Muhlenburg, Philadelphia, 1931, Vol. IV, pp. 9 ff.). His argument is thus very parallel to that of the Anabaptists on the oath. A more likely view is that "unbelief" is synonymous with "worldly," and the reference is rather to guilds and social clubs. Zwingli translates with *foedera*, "covenants." Bullinger bears out this interpretation by reprimanding the Anabaptists at length (*Von dem unverschampten Fräfel. . . ,* pp. cxxi to cxxviii) for their opposition to associations and societies (*pündtnussen und gselschafften*), concord and friendship (*vertrag unnd fründtschafft*) with unbelievers, and seemly temporal joy (*zymliche zytliche fröud*). The later printed text changed *Burgschaft* to *Bürgerschaft* (citizenship), which is less in place in Art. IV. In April 1527 Zwingli was unsure what it meant but leaned toward "serving as a guarantor" (Z, IX, p. 112); by August when he wrote the *Elenchus* he interpreted it as "citizenship," perhaps as referring to the Anabaptists' refusal to perform the citizen's oath. But if *Bürgerschaft* should mean citizenship, the "commitments of unbelief" still must mean some kind of involvement, legal, economic, or social, with unbelievers (Z, VI, p. 121). Lk. 16:15's reference to "abominations" may be alluded to.

65. The printed version adds "doubtless."

66. The printed version reads "unchristian and."

67. Mt. 5:39.

68. 1 Tim. 3:7. Interpreters are not clear where the focus of Art. V lies. Its first thrust is a call for the shepherd to be a morally worthy person, i.e., a critique of the practice of his being appointed on the grounds of his education or social connections without regard to moral stature. Zwingli's translation moves the accent by translating "the shepherd should be one from the congregation," i.e., not someone from elsewhere. As Zwingli knew, the Anabaptists also rejected the naming of a minister to a parish by a distant city council, and he let that knowledge influence his translation.

69. The printed version adds, "to lead the brothers and sisters in prayer, to begin to break bread. . . ."

70. 1 Cor. 9:14.

71. The change in number here from "a shepherd" to "if they sin" is explained by the fact that this sentence is a quotation from 1 Tim. 5:20.

72. "Cross" is already by this time a very clear cliche or "technical term" designating martyrdom.

73. Perhaps "installed" would be less open to the sacramental misunderstanding. *Verordnet* has no sacramental meaning.

74. "Law" here is a specific reference to the Old Testament. Significantly the verb here is not *verordnet* but merely *geordnet;* conveying even less of a sense of permanence or of specific divine institution. It should be noted that in this entire discussion "sword" refers to the judicial and police powers of the state; there is no reference to war in Art. VI; there had been a brief one in IV.

75. "Without the death of the flesh" is the clear reading of the earliest manuscript. Zwingli, however, understood it "toward the putting to death of the flesh," a possible allusion to 1 Cor. 5; the difference in the original is only between *a* and *o*.

76. Mt. 11:29.

77. Jn. 8:11.

78. Jn. 8:22.

79. Lk. 12:13.

80. Two interpretations are possible for "did not discern the ordering of His Father." This may mean that Jesus did not respect, as being an obligation for Him, the service in the state in the office of king, even though the existence of the state is a divine ordinance. More likely would be the interpretation that Jesus did not evaluate the action of the people wanting to make Him king as having been brought about (ordered) by His Father.

81. Mt. 16:24.

82. Mt. 20:25.

83. Rom. 8:30.

84. 1 Pet. 2:21.

85. Phil. 3:20.

86. Here the printed version adds Mt. 12:25: "For every kingdom divided against itself will be destroyed." The reference to solidarity with Christ as Head echoes directly points 4 ff. of the Strasbourg letter.

87. Mt. 12:25.

88. Mt. 5:34-37.

89. Heb. 6:7 ff.

90. Mt. 5:35.

91. Zwingli's translation fills in the argument here: "if it is bad to swear, or even to use the Lord's name to confirm the truth, then the apostles Peter and Paul sinned: for they swore."

92. Lk. 2:34.

93. The difference in tense between "taught" and "says" is in the original; it results from the fact that Scripture references are always given in the present: "Christ says," "Paul says," "Peter says."

94. This concludes the *Seven Articles*.

95. *Vereinigt*.

96. A second reference to 2 Cor. 6:17.

97. Tit. 2:11-14.

98. 24 February.

99. This document has no title; the title chosen here reflects the label given it in the (modern) table of contents of the volume of archival materials UP 80 in the State Archive of Bern. No earlier full translation into English has been published; the text has been digested by Delbert Gratz, *Bernese Anabaptists*, Scottdale, 1953, p. 25, and by Robert Friedmann, *MQR*, 1955, p. 162. Jean Seguy published a translation and commentary in *Christ Seul* (journal of the French Mennonites) No. 1 (p. 13) and No. 2 (p. 5), 1967. The text seems to be in the same hand as the copy of the *Seven Articles*, so that it may be assumed to have circulated together with them and been seized at the same time. (Cf. p. 32.)

100. May mean either: "in the providence of God the Word is preached to us," whereby "Ordnung" would refer to the workings of God in bringing about Reformation and gospel preaching; or "the Word of God is preached according to the divine pattern," with the emphasis on the rediscovery of the true divinely willed church order. The following "whereby" may accordingly refer either to the preaching or to the proper ordering.

101. 1 Jn. 2:8.

102. *Sich üben:* perhaps includes an element of rote learning of gospel narrative and teaching, since literacy and the possession of Bibles was still rare.

103. "Read" includes exposition. "Readings" had been one of the earliest names given to the study meetings held in Zürich and St. Gall prior to the foundation of Anabaptist congregations.

104. "The one to whom God has given the best understanding shall explain it" may mean that, for every particular passage, whoever understands its meaning should speak up. Then we would have a picture of a meeting with no settled leadership, with no controlling role for the "shepherd" who was called for by Schleitheim Article V. Then one might infer, as does Jean Seguy, that this text testifies to a time before the Schleitheim decisions, when congregations functioned without a named leader. It is, however, also possible that "the one to whom God has given the best understanding" may be a circumlocution for a spontaneously recognized leader in the local group.

105. This "reading" may well be rote recitation. This reference to the Psalter is one of the very rare early Anabaptist references to non-congregational devotional exercises. It may be a further trace (see above p. 25 note 19) of an inheritance from monasticism.

106. 1 Tim. 2:8.

107. Mt. 18:15, cf. above note 50.

108. The common fund is seen here as a special purse for specific needs, not as a total communism of consumption such as was established not much later in Moravia. It is significant that the non-Hutterian Anabaptists also considered themselves to be following the economic example of the early Jerusalem Christians.

109. Rom. 14:17. The assumption that the congregation would frequently gather around a simple meal may be linked to their avoidance of social clubs and guilds (above p. 38, Art. IV.

110. The Lord's Supper, specifically identified as such, is evidently distinguished from the rest of the meal, even though both were practiced as often as the brothers met. (Cf. Art. 1).

III

Imprisonment: Letter to Horb

Introduction

Sattler's capture at Horb seems to have taken place immediately upon his return from Schleitheim. Probably the existence of the congregation there had come to light during his absence and his captors were lying in wait for him. Matthias Hiller of St. Gall and Wilhelm Reublin were with him. Reublin escaped but his wife, like Sattler's, was taken captive. Because the population and the city authorities at Horb sprang to the defense of Sattler, the prisoners were moved under heavy guard to a prison in the distant village of Binsdorf, and held there until just before the trial. There he wrote the present letter to the congregation at Horb.

This writing, after the letter to the Strasbourg Reformers, is the only one in the present collection which is undeniably from the pen of Sattler alone and which has a clear epistolary form whereby we can know the addressee. It demonstrates something of the quality of the pastoral concern of Sattler for his churches. It is our best source of insight into the kind of ministry he exercised in South Germany between his departure from Strasbourg and the Schleitheim meeting. It includes as well clear indications of the significance which he ascribed to the Schleitheim decisions.

The Text
Letter to the Church at Horb

To the Church of God at Horb, My Beloved Brothers and Sisters in the Lord[1]

May grace and mercy from God the heavenly Father through Jesus Christ our Lord, and the power of Their Spirit, be with you, brothers and sisters, beloved of God. I cannot forget you although I am not present in the body,[2] but constantly am in care and watching over you as my fellow members, so that not one might ever be drawn away and robbed from the body, whereby the entire body with all its members would be saddened, especially now, as the fury of the tearing wolf has risen most high and has become most powerful, so that he also challenged me to fight with him; but to God be eternally the praise, his head has been split greatly, I hope, his entire body will soon no longer be, as stands written in 4 Esdras 11.[3]

Dear brothers and sisters, you know with what zeal and love I admonished you recently when I was with you, that you would be sincere and righteous in all patience and love of God, so that you can be recognized in the midst of this adulterous generation[4] of godless men, like bright and shining lights which God the heavenly Father has kindled with the knowledge of Him and the light of the Spirit. With that same zeal I now pray and exhort you, that you might walk surely and circumspectly toward those who are without[5] as unbelievers, so that in no way our office which God has laid upon us might be shamed or justifiably mocked.[6] Remember the Lord who gave you a coin (for He will again require the same with interest), lest that one talent be taken away from you. Place it at interest according to the command of the Lord[7] who entrusted it to you. I testify to you by the grace of God that you are valiant and that you walk as befits and becomes the saints of God.[8] Give heed how the Lord rewards lazy servants, namely the lazy and tired hearts, clumsy and cold in the love of God and the brothers; you have experienced what I write you.

Let this be a warning to you lest you receive the same punishment from God.[9] Guard, guard yourselves against such, so that you do not also learn their abominations, who act against the command and law of God, but admonish the

The town of Binsdorf to which Michael Sattler was taken while awaiting trial.

Horb on the Neckar, site of an early Anabaptist fellowship which Michael Sattler served as pastor.

same with strict attentiveness and excommunication according to the command of Christ,[10] yet with all love and compassion for their coldness of heart.[11] If you do this, you will soon see where among the wolves the sheep of God dwell, and will see a quick and rapid separation of those who do not wish to walk the surefooted and living way of Christ, namely through cross, misery, imprisonment, self-denial, and finally through death; thereby you can assuredly present yourselves to God your heavenly Father as a purely righteous, upright congregation of Christ, purified through His blood, that she might be holy and irreproachable before God and men, separated and purified from all idolatry and abomination, so that the Lord of all lords might dwell among them and [that she might] be a tabernacle to Him.[12]

Dear brothers, note what I write, whether it is of the Lord, and apply yourselves to walk accordingly. Let no one shift your goal,[13] as has hitherto happened to some, but go right on, firm and undeviating, in all patience, that you might not of yourselves make void and set aside the cross which God has laid upon you, which would be counter to the honor and praise of God, and furthermore would break and dissolve His eternal, veritable, righteous and life-giving commandments.

Be not weary if you are chastized by the Lord, for he whom God loves He chastizes,[14] and, like a father, He finds pleasure in His son. What would you undertake if you sought to flee from God? What could help you to escape from Him? Is not God the one who fills heaven and earth?[15] Does He not know every secret of your vain heart and the wantonness of your reins? All that is, is manifest before Him, and nothing is hid from Him. You vain man, where would you flee that God would not see you? Why do you flee the rod of your Father? If you will not be drawn according to the will of your Father, you cannot be an heir to His possessions: why do you prefer a brief and passing rest to the blessed, measured chastisement and discipline (for your salvation) of the Lord? How long will you eat meat from the fatness of

Egypt? How long will you be carnally minded? Flesh passes away and all of its glory, only the Word of the Lord remains eternally.[16]

Dear brothers, note what I write you, for it is needful to you, for you see that there are few who are willing to persevere in the chastisement of the Lord, whereas the majority when they suffer something minor in the flesh, become dull and slack, and no more look upon the Prince of our faith[17] and its perfecter Jesus. So they forget all His commandments and cease to treasure the jewel[18] which the calling of God holds out up above and points to for those who conquer, but rather consider much more valuable and useful this temporal ease which they can see, to the eternal which one must hope for.

There are some, where this is put up to them, who blame God, though most wrongly, as if He were not willing to keep them in His protection. You know whom I mean. Watch out that you do not be partakers with such.[19]

Further, dear fellow members in Christ, you should be admonished not to forget love, without which it is not possible that you be a Christian congregation. You know what love is through the testimony of Paul our fellow brother; he says[20]: Love is patient and kind, not jealous, not puffed up, not ambitious, seeks not its own, thinks no evil, rejoices not in iniquity, rejoices in the truth, suffers everything, endures everything, believes everything, hopes everything. If you understand this text, you will find the love of God and of neighbor. If you love God you will rejoice in the truth and will believe, hope, and endure everything that comes from God. Thereby the shortcomings mentioned above can be removed and avoided. But if you love the neighbor, you will not scold or ban zealously, will not seek your own, will not remember evil, will not be ambitious or puffed up, but kind, righteous, generous in all gifts, humble and sympathetic with the weak and imperfect.[21]

Some brothers, I know who they are, have fallen short of this love. They have not wanted to build up one another in love, but are puffed up and have become useless with vain speculation[22] and understanding of those things which God wants to keep secret to Himself. I do not admonish or reject the grace and revelation of God, but the inflated use of this revelation. What is the use, says Paul, if one speaks with all sorts of tongues of men and angels? And knows all mysteries, wisdom, and has all faith, he says, what is all that worth if the one and only love is not exercised? You have experienced what such puffed up speech and unwisdom[23] have brought to birth. You still see daily their false fruits, whether they have abandoned themselves completely to God.

Let no one shift your goal,[24] which has been set in the letter of the Holy Scripture, which is sealed by the blood of Christ and of many witnesses of Jesus. Do not listen what they say from their father, for he is a deceiver,[25] believe not their spirit, for it is completely submerged in the flesh. Judge what I write you, take the matter to heart, so that this abomination may be separated from you and you might be found to be the humble, fruitful, and obedient children of God.

Brothers, wonder not that I deal with the matter thus seriously, for it does not happen without a reason. You have probably learned from brothers how some of ours have been taken prisoner and then, when the brothers had also been taken prisoner in Horb, how we were taken to Binsdorf. During this time we underwent all sorts of attacks from the adversaries. They menaced us once with a cord, then with fire, then with the sword. In such dangers I completely abandoned myself to the Lord in His will and readied myself for death for the sake of His testimony, with all my brothers and my wife.[26] Then I thought of the great number of false brothers and of you who are so few, yea, such a small band; and how few faithful workers there are in the vineyard of the Lord.[27] So it seemed needful to me to urge you by this exhortation to follow us[28] in God's combat and thereby to console you that you might not become weary under the discipline of the Lord.

In sum: dear brothers and sisters, this letter shall be my

Michael Sattler's letter to the congregation at Horb in the Sammelband at Goshen.

farewell from all of you who truly love and follow God (I do not know the others[29]), and a testimony of my love toward you, which God has put in my heart for the sake of your salvation. I would have desired, and, I might hope, it would have been useful, that I had been able to continue for a little time longer to work at the Lord's task, but it is better for my sake to be released and with Christ to await the hope of the blessed. The Lord can certainly raise up for Himself another laborer to complete His work. Pray that reapers may be driven out into the harvest,[30] for the time of threshing has come near. The abomination of desolation is visible among you. The elect servants and maidservants of God will be marked on the forehead with the name of their Father.[31] The world has arisen against those who are redeemed from its error. The gospel is testified to before all the world for a testimony. According to this the day of the Lord must no longer tarry.[32]

You know, my beloved fellow members, how it is fitting to live godly and Christianly. Look out, watch and pray, that your wisdom might not bring you under judgment. Persevere in prayer, that you might stand worthily before the Son of Man. Be mindful of your predecessor,[33] Jesus Christ, and follow after Him in faith and obedience, love and longsuffer-

61

ing. Forget what is carnal, that you might truly be named Christians and children of the most high God; persevere in the discipline of your heavenly Father, and turn not aside, neither to the left, nor to the right, that you might enter in through the gate, and that it might not be needful for you to follow an alien path, which the sinners, sorcerers, idolaters, and everyone who loves and does lies, must take. Be mindful of our meeting, and what was decided there, and continue in strict accordance therewith.[34] And if something should have been forgotten, pray the Lord for understanding. Be generous toward all who have need among you, but especially for those who work among you with the Word and are hunted, and cannot eat their own bread in peace and quiet. Forget not the assembly,[35] but apply yourselves to coming together constantly and that you may be united[36] in prayer for all men and the breaking of bread, and this all the more fervently, as the day of the Lord draws nearer. In such meeting together you will make manifest the heart of the false brothers, and will be freed of them more rapidly.[37]

Lastly, dear brothers and sisters, sanctify yourselves to Him who has sanctified you, and hear what Esdras says:[38] "Await your Shepherd, for He will give you the rest of eternity, for He is near, who will come at the end of the world; be ready for the recompense of the kingdom! Leave the shadows of this world, rise up and stand and behold the number of the marked ones at the supper of the Lord, for those who have separated themselves from the shadow of the world, have received shining clothing from the Lord. O Zion, take again thy number[39] and keep the reckoning of those who have fulfilled the Law of the Lord, for the number of the children whom thou hast desired is completed. On Mount Zion I saw a great host, whom no one can count, and they all praised God with song. In the midst of this host was a young man, taller in stature than all of them, who laid crowns on some of their heads, and was most majestic; I wondered and said to the angel, 'Lord, who are these?' He said: 'These are they who have taken off the mortal robe and drawn on the immortal, and have confessed the name of God. Now they are crowned and receive victory.' I said to the angel, 'Who is this young man who crowns them and gives the victory into their hands?' He said, 'This is the Son of God, whom they confessed in the world. Thus I praised those who stood bravely for the sake of the name of the Lord.' "

Be warned, most beloved members of the body of Christ, of what I point to with such Scripture, and live accordingly, if I am sacrificed to the Lord; may my wife be commended to you as myself.[40] May the peace of Jesus Christ, and the love of the heavenly Father and the grace of Their Spirit keep you flawless, without sin, and present you joyous and pure before the vision of Their holiness at the coming of our Lord Jesus Christ, that you might be found among the number of the called ones at the supper of the one-essential[41] true God and Savior Jesus Christ, to whom be eternally praise and honor and majesty. Amen.

Guard yourselves against false brothers for the Lord will perhaps call me, so now you have been warned. I wait upon my God. Pray without ceasing for all prisoners. May God be with you all, Amen.

In the tower at Binsdorf.

Brother Michael Sattler of Stauffen, together with my fellow prisoners in the Lord.

Notes

1. Köhler, p. 317. In addition to its place in the original pamphlet (see above p. 4), this letter was reprinted in later martyrologies, such as the *Martyrs Mirror*, "*Güldene Aepffel in Silbern Schalen*" (1742) and again in *MGB*, Vol. XIV, 1957, pp. 27 ff.

2. 1 Cor. 5:3.

3. The earliest Anabaptists included the Old Testament Apocrypha in their Scripture study. The picture in *4 Esdras* (*2 Esdras* in modern numbering) chap. 11 is of an eagle which rises up out of the sea and then is destroyed. It is not clear whether the replacement of the eagle by a wolf in Sattler's reference comes from a fusion of this image with other New Testament pictures of the wolf as symbol of the threat of dangerous religious leaders (Acts 20:29) or whether some variant manuscript might actually have had a wolf in the *Esdras* passage.

4. Mk. 8:38. The next line is an allusion to Phil. 2:15 ff.

5. Eph. 5:15; 1 Tim. 3:7.

6. It is not clear whether "our office which God has laid upon us" is a reference to

the particular calling and reputation of Michael Sattler or to the calling of all Christians. Since elsewhere in the letter Sattler speaks directly of himself in the first person singular, it is more likely that here "us" refers to all Christians.

7. Mt. 25:14, 27.

8. The word here translated "testified" is *bezeug*. It would seem more appropriate for Sattler to be saying here "I exhort you" or "I adjure you": but the word cannot normally be given such a meaning.

9. The last two sentences must refer to some sort of "punishment" which had befallen some other leaders in the radical Reformation movement whose devotion was "lazy." These unnamed persons are probably parallel to the "false brothers" referred to in the cover letter of the *Schleitheim Confession* (above p. 35). The "punishment" would seem to refer not to discipline by the congregation but rather to some other fate which befell those leaders, whether at the hands of government, by illness, or by personal moral breakdown, in such a way that Sattler can consider it an evidence of divine judgment.

10. "Command of Christ" or "Rule of Christ" is a standard designation for the imperative of Mt. 18:15 ff.

11. Cf. note 21 below.

12. 2 Cor. 6:17; Rev. 21:3.

13. Col. 2:18. This is a favorite text of Sattler's. *Katabrabeuein* is translated "disqualify" by RSV, following the most literal sense of the verb as designating an unfavorable ruling by an umpire (*brabeus*). The rendering "take away the prize for the race" (from *brabeia*, the palm or wand awarded the winner) follows the Vulgate. The prize may be taken away by deceit (KJV, "beguile") or by a just action of an umpire (because someone else won the race) or by someone usurping the umpire's function. Each of these images puts in a slightly different light the work of the false prophet. Sattler cites Luther's rendering, "das Ziel verrücken," but probably also has in mind the meaning of the Latin. His meaning is thus probably, "let no one distract you from reaching your goal"; the false prophet is seen as keeping one from reaching the goal by moving the goal.

14. Heb. 12:6.

15. Gen. 14:19? Jer. 23:24? Ps. 139? The remainder of this paragraph gathers a profusion of biblical images and allusions which, however, cannot be all identified with particular texts.

16. 1 Pet. 1:24.

17. Gal. 2:10; Heb. 12:2?

18. This "jewel" might be the pearl of great price in Jesus' parable or the "stone" of Rev. 2:17; more likely the latter.

19. This reference to false brothers together with the phrase "you know whom I mean" is in direct parallel to the cover letter to the *Schleitheim Confession* and thereby reinforces the probability of Sattler's authorship of that cover letter. It is significant that these unfaithful persons attributed their deviant behavior to divine leading or Providence. This as well would parallel the indication in the Schleitheim cover letter that the "false brothers" described their excesses as "Christian liberty."

20. The phrase *Mit bruder* is striking. Does it imply a polemic against the glorification of the apostles as saints? Or is it a testimony to the Anabaptist leaders' sense of contemporaneity with the apostles in the restoration of the New Testament church?

21. Sattler's call for love and patience in the exercise of discipline is most significant, in view of recent tendencies to interpret Sattler and Schleitheim as advocates of a legalistic view of discipline. (See above p. 31.)

22. "*Wissenheit*," i.e., knowingness, gnosis.

23. "*Unwissenheit*." This is not the mystical glorification of "unknowing" as an

especially profound kind of insight, but a mocking reversal of the claim to special inspiration. The allusion to 1 Cor. 13:1 f. claims apostolic precedent for the same depreciation of special claims.

24. Cf. note 13 above. The frequency of quotation of this phrase is testimony to the disciplined purposiveness of Sattler's vision of the Christian life.

25. Jn. 8:44.

26. The phrase used by the Anabaptists to refer to their wives was "eheliche schwester" or "marital sister." (Cf. below pp. 77, 79 f.) This usuage testifies to the Anabaptist conviction that Christian commitment is prior to marital commitment. What matters about one's wife is first of all that she is a sister, a Christian, committed believer in her own right; that is the noun. What matters second is that she is married; this is the adjective.

27. Mt. 9:37? Mt. 20?

28. The verb "*nachfolgen*" can be used indiscriminately for the call to imitate the preacher or to follow Christ or God. It is applied in this sentence to Sattler himself and in the next to God. Cf. 1 Cor. 11:1.

29. It is not clear whether "I do not know" indicates that Sattler is not personally *acquainted* with the particular false leaders in question or simply that he does not *recognize* them as the addressees of this letter. The verb *erkennen* can have either sense.

30. Mt. 9:38. The verb "drive" is a striking statement of the Anabaptist sense of mission.

31. Rev. 7:3.

32. Mt. 24:14?

33. 1 Pet. 2:21? Heb. 12:1 ff.?

34. "Our meeting" might conceivably be a reference to the Schleitheim gathering and its conclusions. This would then indicate how rapidly Schleitheim took on a normative character. It would also indicate that numerous other members of the Horb congregation had been at Schleitheim. Another possible interpretation would relate this allusion to some other gathering at Horb in which that congregation had made decisions which Sattler calls them now to live up to. Also in this case it is of theological significance that a leader calls for faithfulness to the conclusions reached by the brotherhood *at a past meeting*, rather than appealing to a law, to his credentials, to a Bible text, etc.

35. Heb. 10:25.

36. "*Vereinigt.*" We noted the importance of this term in the Schleitheim text (text pp. 35 ff.; notes 31, 36 f., 45, 52 f., 59).

37. Sattler places great trust in the local meeting not only to find guidance and establish truth but also to unveil the false brothers.

38. *4 Esdras* 2:34-37. Other Scripture references listed above in footnotes have been unmarked allusions. Here Sattler both labels the source in his text and quotes the long passage.

39. Literally "keep your chalk." Walter Köhler in his annotation suggests that the reference here is to whiteness, pointing out the parallel to the Vulgate term "candidatos" which also has this meaning. This would then call for a specific allusion to a picture of the multitude of the elect in bright white robes. More likely, however, the meaning is revealed by ordinary Hebrew parallelism, making simply another reference (as in the English "to chalk up") to counting, so that "take again thy number" and "keep the reckoning" are identical in meaning.

40. I.e., take care of her as you would of me. This indicates that Sattler was expecting to be executed himself but thought his wife would be released.

41. What we have translated as "one-essential" is the technical term "eingewesen," which was the translation for *homoousios*, the Nicene term for the identity of essence of the Son with the Father.

IV

Martyrdom

Introduction

Of four or five known contemporary reports of the trial and execution of Sattler, three have been preserved. We here reproduce in its entirety the version which found its place in the early pamphlet collection,[1] adding piecemeal from the others such elements as complement its account.[2]

Since the texts themselves are narrative in character, we here omit the recounting of the events they record,[3] limiting our reporting to the developments before and after the trial.

The Austrian government had considerable difficulty in getting the trial under way. The Council at Horb refused to take responsibility for the proceedings. Another court therefore had to be constituted in the name of the Count of Hohenburg, Joachim of Zollern. Originally the date was set for March 18 but it had to be postponed twice. The chief difficulty was in finding judges for such an *ad hoc* proceeding in which it was taken for granted that the result would be a death penalty. The nearby cities of Ueberlingen, Villingen, Radolfzell and Stockach, and the universities of Tübingen and Freiburg were asked to send two judges each. The universities refused, perhaps partly because of moral revulsion at the thought of such a condemnation, perhaps partly because they knew the execution would be unpopular among the people, but also on the solid legal grounds that all of their doctors of canonical and civil law were priests or candidates for the priesthood. Having participated in a trial whose result was the death penalty would, according to the ruling of the Fourth Lateran Council (1215), disqualify priests for ordination or for the exercise of their office. Finally, under the pressures of governmental insistence and the promise of increased expenses money, two lay representatives were found from each of the universities, but in neither case did they represent the faculty of law.

The echo of the execution of Sattler was rapid and widespread. We shall observe (Text V) the disapproval of the city fathers of Horb and the Reformers of Strasbourg. The action was not made more acceptable by the leading role which was played in the trial by the representatives of the tyrannical Ensisheim administrators of the Austrian Empire. The almost immediate circulation of the report in several printed versions testifies to the wide extent of popular interest in this martyrdom. In its turn the publication contributed to giving to Sattler's death a unique place in Anabaptist memory. He is the only martyr from South Germany whose story has been taken up into the Dutch Mennonite martyrologies, and the first whose story is told at any length in the Hutterian *Chronicles*. He is not the first Anabaptist martyr, nor was the manner of his execution the most cruel. The special place which this execution holds in the memories of early Anabaptism is largely a testimony to the personal stature which he had acquired, well beyond the confines of the particular congregations he served, as the spiritual pillar of the Swiss Brethren movement.

The Text
Trial and Martyrdom

A. Preface to the Account of Klaus von Graveneck [1]

Since in these last most dangerous times, when (thanks be to God) the light of divine truth has gone forth, and shines so brightly that it makes manifest the abominable error of the anti-Christ and shines into the thick darkness of false doc-

Rottenburg on the Neckar, where the trial against Sattler and members of his congregation was conducted.

trine, and thereby takes away from the enemy of man's salvation that which he had seized, destroys his kingdom, and [since] the kingdom of Christ is gaining ground, now the strong warrior, of whom Christ spoke in Luke 11 [v. 21] becomes active, readies himself for defense, uses all his evil ruses, creates sects and division, which he lets be decorated and colored by his chosen worldly wise and skillful workers and servants, so beautifully that, if at all possible, the elect servants of God might be seduced, as Christ in Matthew 24 [v. 24] predicted as a warning to us. And such has God the Father in heaven permitted to happen to His believers, that they might be tested, tried and made manifest, as Paul writes in 1 Corinthians 11 [v. 9,] "There must be division among you, so that they who are genuine may be made manifest."

So it seemed good to us to make known in print this authentic and wonderful story and report the trustworthy persons herein named, so that many might see how God so marvelously deals with His saints here, and tests them as gold through fire, that is, with manifold temptation and testing, as

The approximate site on the Neckar River along the old road to Tübingen, where Michael Sattler was burned at the stake on May 20, 1527.

it stands in 1 Peter 1 [v. 7], so that everyone might use and strengthen his faith, might not let himself be turned away from the bright and clear Word of God by any kind of miraculous signs or seemingly beautiful doctrine, but should hold fast thereto with solid faith, until God lets him see into all truth.

Whereunto the apostle already named faithfully admonishes us [2 Pet. 1:19] as he speaks, "We have a solid prophetic word, and you do well to pay attention to it as to a light which shines in a dark place, until the day breaks and the morning star rises in your hearts." May the Father of light grant this to all of us and illuminate us with the light of His divine truth. Amen.

B. Following are the Articles and Proceedings which Michael Sattler attested with his blood at Rottenburg on the Neckar[5]

After various formalities (on the day of his departure from this world[6]), since the points of accusation were many, Michael Sattler requested that they might be read back to him and that he might be heard thereon; against which the *Schultheiss* (as the advocate of his lord⁷) objected and did not wish to grant. Michael thereupon asked for a ruling. When the judges had taken counsel, the answer was that, insofar as the prosecution would be willing to permit this, the judges would find it proper. Thereupon the *Stadtschreiber* of Ensisheim, as speaker of the said advocate,⁸ spoke as follows: "Provident, honorable, and wise lords, he has boasted that he has the Holy Spirit, therefore it would seem to me not to be necessary to grant him this; for if he has the Holy Spirit, as he boasts, the Spirit should be able to tell him what is in the indictment."⁹

To this Michael Sattler answered: "Ye servants of God, I hope that this will not be denied to me; for the stated points of accusation do not all concern me and I do not know what they are."

Answer of the *Stadtschreiber:* "Provident, honorable, and wise lords, although we are not obligated to do so, we are willing out of generosity to concede this to him, so that, in his heresy, it may not be thought that he has been subjected to injustice or that anyone desires to be unfair to him, therefore let the articles be read again to him orally." The following are the articles:

1. That he and his associates¹⁰ have acted against imperial mandate.¹¹

2. He has taught, held, and believed, that the body and blood of Christ are not in the sacrament.

3. He taught and believes that infant baptism is not requisite toward salvation.

4. They have rejected the sacrament of unction.

5. Despised and scorned the mother of God and the saints.

6. They have said that one should not swear to the government.

7. Initiated a new and unheard-of usage in the Lord's Supper, with wine and bread crumbled in a basin, and eating the same.¹²

8. He has forsaken the order and has married a wife.

9. He has said: "If the Turk were to come into the land, one should not resist him, and, if it were right to wage war, he would rather go to war against the Christians than against the Turks," which is after all a great offense, to take the side of the greatest enemy of our holy faith against us.

Whereupon Michael Sattler requested that he might be able to consult with his brothers and sisters; this was granted to him.[13] When he had spoken with them only a short time, he took the floor and answered fearlessly thus:

Concerning the articles which have to do with me, my brothers and sisters, hear the following brief statement:

1. We do not admit that we have acted counter to the imperial mandate; for it says that one should not adhere to the Lutheran doctrine and seduction, but only to the gospel and the Word of God;[14] this we have held to.[15] Counter to the gospel and the Word of God I do not know that I have done anything; in witness thereto I appeal to the words of Christ.

2. That the real body of Christ the Lord is not in the sacrament, we admit: for Scripture says:[16] Christ has ascended to heaven and sits at the right hand of His heavenly Father, whence He shall come to judge the living and the dead. It follows therefrom, since He is in heaven and not in the bread, that He cannot be eaten bodily.[17]

3. Regarding baptism we say: infant baptism is not useful toward salvation, for it stands written, that we live only by faith.[18] Further: "He who believes and is baptized, will be saved." Peter says in 1 Peter 3: "which also now saves you in baptism, which[19] thereby signifies not the laying off of filth of the flesh but the covenant of a good conscience with God through the resurrection of Christ."

4. We have not rejected oil, for it is a creature of God. What God has made is good and not to be rejected. But what pope, bishop, monks, and priests have wanted to do to improve on it, this we think nothing of. For the pope has never made anything good. What the epistle of James[20]

speaks of is not the pope's oil.

5. We have not dishonored the mother of God and the saints; rather the mother of Christ is to be praised above all women because to her was given the grace that she could give birth to the Savior of the whole world. That she, however, is a mediatrix and advocate, the Scripture knows nothing of; for she must like us await judgment. Paul says to Timothy[21] that Christ is our mediator and advocate before God. Concerning the saints, we say that we who live and believe are the saints. I testify to this with the epistle of Paul to the Romans, Corinthians, Ephesians, and elsewhere: he always writes: "To the beloved saints." Therefore we, who believe, are the saints. Those who have died in the faith we call the "blessed."[22]

6. We hold that one should not swear allegiance to government[23] for the Lord says in Matthew 5: "You should swear no oath, but your speech shall be yea, yea, nay, nay."

7. When God called me to testify to His Word, and I read Paul, I considered the unchristian and dangerous estate[24] in which I had been, in view of the pomp, pride, usury, and great fornication of the monks and priests.[25] I therefore obeyed and took a wife according to the command of God. Paul was prophesying well on the subject to Timothy: "In the last days it shall come to pass that they will forbid marriage and food,[26] which God has created that they might be enjoyed with thanksgiving."

8. If the Turk comes, he should not be resisted, for it stands written: thou shalt not kill. We should not defend ourselves against the Turks or our other persecutors, but with fervent prayer should implore God that He might be our defense and our resistance. As to me saying that if waging war were proper I would rather take the field against the so-called[27] Christians who persecute, take captive, and kill true Christians, than against the Turks, this was for the following reason: the Turk is a genuine Turk and knows nothing of the Christian faith. He is a Turk according to the flesh. But you claim to be Christians, boast of Christ, and

still persecute the faithful witnesses of Christ. Thus you are Turks according to the Spirit.

To conclude: you servants of God,[28] I admonish you to consider whereto you have been established by God to punish evil, to defend and protect the just. Since, then, we have done nothing counter to God and the gospel, consider therefore what you are doing. You should also ask, and you will find, that I and my brothers and sisters have not acted against any government in words or deeds.

Therefore, you servants of God, in case you might not have heard or read the Word of God, would you send for the most learned [men] and for the godly books of the Bible,[29] in whatever language they might be, and let them discuss the same with us in the Word of God. If they show us with Holy Scripture that we are in error and wrong, we will gladly retract and recant, and will gladly suffer condemnation and the punishment for our offense.[30] But if we cannot be proved in error, I hope to God that you will repent and let yourselves be taught.

After this speech most of the judges laughed and shook their heads. The *Stadtschreiber* of Ensisheim spoke: "O yes, you disreputable, desperate, and mischievous monk, you think we should debate with you? Sure enough, the hangman will debate with you, you can believe me."

Michael: "What God wills, that will come to pass."

Stadtschreiber: "It would have been good if you had never been born."

Michael: "God knows what is good.[31]

Stadtschreiber: "You arch heretic, you have seduced pious people; if they would only give up their errors and ask for grace."

Michael: "Grace is in God alone."

One of the prisoners: "One should not deviate from the truth."

Schultheiss: "You desperate evil doer and arch heretic, I tell you this: if there were no hangmen here I would hang you myself and would be sure I would be serving God thereby."

Michael: "God will judge rightly."

Whereupon the *Stadtschreiber* spoke with him several words in Latin, unknown to me,[32] whereupon Michael answered: "*Indica.*"

So the *Stadtschreiber* asked the judge to give a final verdict: "This kind of talk could go on all day: therefore, Lord Judge, would you proceed with the verdict, I rest the case."

The judge asks Michael Sattler if he also rests.

He spoke: "You servants[33] of God, I have not been sent to defend the Word of God in court. We are sent to testify thereto. Therefore we cannot consent to any legal process, for we have no such command from God.[34] If, however, we have not been able to be justly convinced, we are ready to suffer, for the Word of God, whatever will and may be laid upon us to suffer, all for our faith in Christ Jesus our Savior, as long as we have in us a breath of life, unless we should be convinced otherwise with Scripture."

Stadtschreiber: "The hangman will prove it to you, he can debate with you, arch heretic."

Michael: "I appeal[35] to Scripture."

Whereafter the judges arose, went into another room, and remained there perhaps an hour and a half to reach their verdict. Meanwhile some in the courtroom handled Michael miserably, mocked him, one of them saying: "If I see that you get out of this, I'll believe in you.[36] How could you mislead yourself and these others and seduce them in this way?" Drawing at the same time a sword which had been lying on the table, he said, "See, with this we will debate with you." But Michael answered nothing concerning his person but bore everything[37] willingly, while one of the prisoners spoke: "Do not throw pearls before swine." When Michael was challenged, why he did not remain a lord in the cloister[38] he answered: "According to the flesh I would be a lord but it is better as it is." He spoke no more words than are recorded here, and spoke these fearlessly.

When then the judges returned to the room the verdict was read, as follows: "In the matter of the prosecutor of the imperial majesty versus Michael Sattler, it has been found that Michael Sattler should be given into the hands of the hangman, who shall lead him to the square and cut off his tongue, then chain[39] him to a wagon, there tear his body twice with red hot tongs, and again when he is brought before the gate, five more times." When this is done to be burned to powder as a heretic.[40]

C. Conclusion of Klaus von Graveneck's Report

All of this I saw and heard myself. May God grant to us as well to testify so courageously and patiently. Amen.

Afterward he was led back to prison until the third day, but first of all into a room where he spoke thus to the *Schultheiss: "Schultheiss,* you know that you and your fellow judges have condemned me contrary to justice and without proof, therefore look out, and repent, for if not, you and they will be eternally condemned before the judgment of God to eternal fire."

Whereafter on May 20 he was led to the marketplace and the judgment which had been pronounced was executed against him. After cutting off his tongue he was chained[41] to the cart and according to the verdict torn with red hot tongs; then burnt in fire. Nevertheless, at first in the square and then again at the place of execution he prayed to God for his persecutors and also encouraged others to pray for them and finally spoke thus: "Almighty eternal God, Thou who art the way and the truth, since I have not been taught otherwise by anyone, so by Thy help I will testify this day to the truth and seal it with my blood." He also exhorted the *Schultheiss* as he had spoken before, he was answered, that he should busy himself with God. When he had commended his spirit to God he was thrown on the frame into the fire, and immediately the bands on his hands opened and he gave the agreed sign with both hands;[42] thus he longsufferingly died.[43]

Whereafter their verdict was also announced to their brothers, of whom there were twelve men and ten women, as follows: first concerning two old men, one of whom had recanted, it was ruled that their tongues should be split and henceforth for a whole year they should stand at the church door every Sunday when the bells ring, holding in their hand a wooden image of a font.

Another, one of them named Veyt Feringer, who in his fear had been the first to apostasize and had recanted, and had offered to believe everything his government wanted, the judgment was that he should first be beheaded and then burned.

Third, a young man of about fifteen or sixteen years was condemned to eternal prison. The others shall all be burned alive as heretics.

Fifth, the women shall all be drowned, except for one young one who was pregnant. They should wait with her until after the birth, when she should also be executed.

This court had been gathered together from many places, namely from Tübingen two young doctors of law, two from the Council of Ueberlingen on the Lake of Constance, two from Freiburg in the Breisgau, two from Ensisheim two from Villingen, two from Stockach, two from Ehingen, two from Rottenburg.

The Count of Zollern, as Lord of the province of Hohenburg, had proposed to them that they should commit themselves by oath that without regard for any conditions, favors, gifts, envy, commands, or whatever they would judge freely according to justice, Christianly and sincerely. They refused this oath and answered that they would stand by the oaths which they had spoken to their [respective] lords at home.

They had previously been in prison for thirteen weeks and on Friday before *Cantate* had been brought before the court and accused as was said above. Then three had recanted. One of them, Veyt Feringer, finally retracted his recantation, wherefor his life was also condemned. May God grant to them all eternal rest, and to us that we in our last hours may all be found in a genuine, solid Christian faith. Amen.

D. Conclusion of Wilhelm Reublin's Report of Sattler's Trial and Death[44]

To these accusations Michael answered himself with mild, Christian speech, about each and every article, grounding and supporting himself only upon the one eternal Word of God in Old and New Testaments. And if he should be refuted therefrom [from Scripture] he would be ready to suffer punishment. If, however, he could establish and bring forth [his position] with divine words and truth, he should properly be freed and remain unpunished etc. He asked for the Bible, for scholars, and for all Christians on earth, before whom he would be ready to give an account of his faith. Insistently he called for Scripture to be judge. But this was not to be.

To which the Lord Advocate, the *Stadtschreiber* of Ensisheim, said: "The hangman is the one who should debate with him." Drawing his sword half out of its sheath, he said, "If he does not, then I myself will execute you with this sword. And thereby would do God a service." With which he rested his case.

But Michael would not argue the case, but was rather ready to suffer [which he said] in a clear Christian way, and commended himself to God and His will.

The judgment which was given: that Michael should be led to the market, his tongue be cut off and then gripped six times with red hot tongs, be thrown alive into a fire and burnt to a powder.

Whereupon [immediately after the pronouncing of the verdict] he joyfully addressed and consoled his wedded sister[45] in the presence of the lords and princes.

Then he was put back in the prison from Saturday till Monday. (What anxiety, combat, and strife his flesh and spirit had with one another is inconceivable. What he in his love must have meditated.[46]) And then on the said day, according to the content of the verdict, he was led out and they began by cutting off his tongue and tearing his body with red hot tongs. But he praised God at the place of execution, hard and strong. As he was being tied to the ladder with cords, he admonished the *Schultheiss* that he should meditate on the words which he had spoken with him in love and secretly, and that he should willingly render himself to God the Lord.[47]

A small sack of powder was hung around his neck and thus he was thrown into the fire.[48] When then the powder went off and one despaired of his still being alive, he cried with a clear voice often and constantly to God in heaven. When he had been crying thus for a long time, he became unbound in the fire[49] and raised his arms high with the first two fingers on each hand outstretched and cried with a powerful voice: "Father, into thy hands I commend my soul!" And thus ended his life. The Lord be eternally praised. Amen! His right hand could not be burned up, nor the heart, until the executioner had to cut it into pieces, and then the blood at first spurted high heavenward. In the night, many observed the sun and the moon standing still above the place of execution, three hours long, with golden letters written within. Such a bright light went out from them that many thought it was midday. Which the rulers undertook to forbid and suppress with oaths. Which, however, was no help.[50]

Four others, namely Mathias Kursiner, Stefel Schumacher, Schibel Lentzi, and the elder Giger[51] were also led out the evening of the same day and likewise persevered Christian and firm in the faith and in the divine Word and belief, and spoke Christianly and consolingly to one another. Just when they came to the place of execution a messenger came on horseback and spoke to them (in a very considerate way) that if they would be ready to recant they were amnestied by the grace of the countess. They answered that they prefer the grace of God to human grace "and our life should not hinder us in this, nor any of the goods of this world." And with joyful hearts they kneeled down and their heads were struck off. Mathias was once more pressed, when the other three lay dead before him, that he should now save his life, recant and ask for mercy, and he would live, he said very quickly, "No, God forbid. If I had seven heads I would hold them all out for the sake of the name of Christ." He knelt, and commended his soul into the hand of God. And thus their lives ended.

On Wednesday Michael's wife was taken out on the waters of the Neckar. She could not be turned away from her faith by any human grace or words.[52] In great joy and strong faith she accepted and suffered death. God be praised! Thus she was drowned.

The other women and men all recanted at Rottenburg and abjured with two fingers laid in a Bible, and swore an oath: that the blood and flesh of Jesus Christ are in the sacrament of the altar, etc., further that infant baptism is right, etc. And that they hold and believe what the Roman church has established, and that it is correct, and they wish to fulfill it. And on each of them a gray coat was put on, with a chalice and host painted on the breast and a font on the other side; they swore to leave the land and not to remain there overnight. Agreed further that they wished truthfully to confess that they were in error.

There were fourteen more who, it was also ruled, should be accepted.[53]

It also happened during Lent that four brothers were imprisoned in a dungeon in Rottenburg and with a bread knife broke through a wall and from there up through fourteen feet of solid ground. One of these also recanted, by name Martin Schülle, who had previously been frivolous about it and who had to confess his error in writing. Which was read out to the other brothers and brought it about, in the knowledge of the verdict against Michael, that some others recanted.[54]

E. Valerius Anshelm's Chronicle Report on Michael Sattler's Death[55]

He had been prior at St. Peter's in the Black Forest. He said to the scolding accuser: "Who do you think you are? A gray coat will hardly make the difference. You too will find a just judge. May He be more gracious to you than you are to those who confess His name."

His wife had been a beguine, such a refined and comely little woman that the wife of the imperial regent, the Countess of Hohenzollern, undertook to draw her away from her confession and to keep her alive, keeping her in her court. This was useless, for she persisted in saying that the crown she wanted was the one her Lord Jesus would give, and that she wished to hold Christianly the pledge which she had spoken to her Christian husband. On the eighth day she courageously let herself be taken to the Neckar and be drowned. She would rather have gone into the fire with her husband. These would have nothing to do with recanting.

The others, driven to a miserable recantation, had to pledge themselves to public penance, as the price of their amnesty to stand for a year in gray coats, on which a chalice and a font of cloth were sewn, bareheaded and barefoot, with rods on their arms, every holiday in front of the parish church at the time of mass and of vespers. A few, including educated priests, had all their property taken and were banned twenty miles out of the land.[56]

Notes

1. Köhler, pp. 325 ff. This text is not the earliest one; it bears the marks of editorial abbreviation (cf. below notes 6 and 40). The present translation is new; it, however, is not substantially different from the version long circulated in the *Martyrs Mirror* translations which came *via* the Dutch, which George H. Williams annotated and included in *SAW*, pp. 136 ff.

2. The Bender/Bossert article in *ME* IV, p. 430, lists five sources; the Hutterian *Chronicle* report, however, is not a fifth, independent version but a brief secondhand summary. In addition to the above sources, Martin Bucer in his *Getrewe Warnung* refers to an account whose author designated himself as "L" and as an eyewitness (Krebs-Rott, *op. cit.*, p. 113, Stupperich, *op cit.*, p. 256). This does not fit any of the other known sources in their extant form, and has not been further identified by scholarship. Bucer wonders whether the witness might be Ludwig Hätzer, and reproaches him for not giving his full name.

3. Numerous unclear details, especially in connection with the capture and movement of the prisoners, their number, the constitution of the court, and the government's pressure on the local authorities, cannot adequately be unraveled without renewed access to sources unavailable in America; these matters are not pursued here.

4. Klaus von Graveneck was a minor Swabian nobleman, a vassal of Joachim, but a Protestant. His presence at the trial was probably not a matter of free choice, but of feudal obligation. His brother-in-law Balthasar Maler was a printer in Zürich and may have done the actual writing. The Graveneck text is used here only insofar as its variants are noted by Köhler and Cramer. As we shall see it is earlier than the Köhler text. Its title page is reproduced in *ML*, IV, p. 32.

5. Here begins the text of the version reproduced by Köhler.

6. This was not the day of Sattler's departure from this world. Here, as below note 40, there is evidence of an editorial telescoping of the account, which makes a one-day narrative out of the trial and the execution. The trial took two days, the verdict was read on Saturday May 18 and the execution was the following Monday or Tuesday.

7. I.e., as prosecutor. "His Lord" is the Holy Roman Emperor, of whose government Ensisheim was the local administrative seat. *Schultheiss* or *Statthalter* is the procurator or regent.

8. The secretary or town clerk of Ensisheim, Eberhard Hoffmann, is thus the speaker or the counsel for the *Schultheiss*.

9. Literally: "What action has been taken." The formal first reading of the indictment had placed the accusations in the record, even if they were read too rapidly for Sattler to be able to remember them in the proper order.

10. The other captives are not on trial here. They are mentioned here as a measure of Sattler's guilt in leading others astray.

11. There was at this time no imperial mandate in effect making Anabaptism an offense. The prosecution must be claiming to apply the edict of Worms (against Luther, May 1521), which, however, does not mention baptism or Anabaptism, and which the empire had given up attempting to put into effect against the Lutherans.

12. This is the one point in the accusation which Sattler did not take up in his defense, at least as this is recorded. Scholars have differed both as to whether the accusation was correct and as to what such a practice would have meant. Walter Köhler (*op. cit.*, p. 293), assumes the accusation was correct, since such a practice is reported from later lower-Rhine Anabaptism, and that it was derived from a literal imitation of the Last Supper (Mt. 26:23). Zürich historian Ulrich Gäbler (in a personal communication) believes that the accusation is correct, and that the usage was parallel to and derived from the Catholic practice of *commixtio*, whereby one fragment of the Host is laid in the Cup to represent the unity of Body and Blood. Gustav Bossert (*ML* IV, p. 33, followed by Bender in *ME* IV, p. 430) considers the accusation to be false, arising from a misunderstanding of the term "breaking of bread." For Williams, "this is an understandable distortion of what the Catholic authorities had been told was a common meal in place of the Mass" (*SAW*, p. 141, note 13).

The circumstantial evidence seems to be against the accusation's being correct: (a) all the other accusations were true; Sattler could justify his convictions biblically but he did not deny holding the position which the prosecution found offensive. If he had agreed that this report was true he would likely also have given his reasons. If on the other hand he had denied this one point (which the prosecution would then not have pursued, since the rest was abundant ground for conviction) it is quite understandable that the eyewitness might have omitted the denial from the record. Or Sattler might have omitted any defense at this point, choosing to testify only at those points where the accusations were relevant. He had said in his first statement that not all the points concerned him. (b) Sattler was deeply involved in and eminently representative of the Swiss Brethren movement in its extension from Zürich to Strasbourg and Augsburg. If by this time he had established any such practice, the likelihood is that we would have some other contemporary witnesses to it. This is a context where the argument from silence has some weight. Schleitheim's imagery of "breaking one loaf" and "drinking one cup" give no hint of such a usage.

This reading of the circumstantial probabilities leaves unexplained how the prosecution, otherwise rather well informed, could have come to include the accusation.

13. Sattler is consulting with his brothers as to whether he should function as their spokesman, and as to whether they wish to defend themselves by judicial argument. Their decision is not to accept the role of defendants. They will state their position and will ask for discussion of the issues before the bar of Scripture, but they will not seek to argue before the court their innocence of the charges. This is partly because of their convictions against judicial self-defense (1 Cor. 6), partly because they are clearly guilty of behaving as charged, and partly because it is not the mandate of governments to rule on church order. Thus what Sattler goes on to say is not an argument for the defense, but a testimony of faith prior to the rejection of judicial procedure. (Cf. below note 30.)

14. The Graveneck report here has "the words of Christ."

15. The Nüremberg Reichstag of 1524, a compromise to get past the Lutheran-Catholic conflict, had commanded that everyone should teach the "holy gospel and the word of God according to a true and correct understanding and exposition of the teachings accepted by the universal church without unrest and scandal." The Reichstag of 1522-23 had ordered that nothing should be taught "except the genuine, pure, clear and holy Gospel . . . according to the teaching and exposition of the writings which have been tested and received by the Christian church." Both these weasel-worded phrases were efforts to avoid the implementation of the anti-Lutheran provisions of the 1521 Edict of Worms. Both were compromise phrasings, and neither had the Anabaptists in mind. In their direct legal meaning, they were superseded in 1526 by new actions of the Reichstag at Speyer. Its intention was a compromise between the two state-church *systems* of the Lutheran and Catholic provinces; it did not mean to speak to the issue of *individual* liberties. Since, however, it avoided condemning specific doctrines and appealed only to the Word of God and the gospel, every dissenter could appeal to it as well.

16. The Dutch translation refers at this point to the texts Eph. 4:8; Acts 1:9; Col. 3:8; Acts 10:22; 2 Tim. 4:1. But what Sattler himself goes on to quote at this point as "Scripture" is in fact from the Apostles' Creed.

17. The Graveneck text here has "wesentlich," i.e., "substantially."

18. Jn. 20:31; Hab. 2:4; Rom. 1:7. The first scriptural proof here is an imprecise allusion to the key Reformation text; the second is a literal quotation without identification of the source (Mk. 16:16), and the third is a full quotation with the source indicated (1 Pet. 3:21). The "covenant of a good conscience" was thus already in early 1527 the key text for the Anabaptist concept of baptism.

19. The Graveneck account here had "the baptism which is indicated by Jesus." This is not the sense of the text which Sattler is here citing from memory, but neither is the entire relative clause with *jenes* ("which thereby signifies") in the printed account. It is thus possible that Sattler intentionally inserted into the 1 Peter quotation the phrase, "which Jesus commands" between "baptism" and "not the laying off. . . ."

20. Jas. 5:14. "The pope's oil" refers to the sacrament of unction.

21. 1 Tim. 2:5.

22. *Selig.*

23. The earliest Anabaptists were divided about the degree of thoroughness with which to apply Jesus' prohibition of the oath. Some, while rejecting both cheap cursing and private asseverations, would still permit an oath of loyalty to government. Sattler thus takes the stricter position.

24. *Stand;* not one's personal condition but his social and vocational "station" or place in society.

25. The Graveneck text here adds "with one of them making a harlot of his wife,

another of his daughter, another of a maid."

26. 1 Tim. 4:3.

27. "So-called" is not in the Graveneck account.

28. Here, as in Sattler's first speech, the allusion to Rom. 13, conflated with 1 Pet. 2:14, is pointed.

29. The Graveneck account has: "the oldest books in the Bible." This appeal to "the oldest Bible" expresses the Anabaptist claim to be not innovating but rather restoring original Christianity. "Oldest" probably means "original."

30. Willingness to suffer even if proved wrong was characteristic of the Anabaptist readiness for debate. Conrad Grebel is a similar way once proposed that if he were to debate with Zwingli and be defeated he should be burned as a heretic, as the old regime demanded, but if he were to win the debate Zwingli should not be burned, since the new insight forbids such sanctions: J. Yoder, *Gespräche*, p. 71.

31. This line is filled in from the Graveneck text. The pamphlet report has only the *Stadtschreiber* in this exchange. This may indicate the priority of the Graveneck text with its greater detail.

32. I.e., the reporter does not understand Latin. Williams suggests that the reason for the recourse to Latin was that the prosecutor felt the audience's displeasure at his bad manners. It is also possible that he was falling back into the normal language for legal technicalities, since Sattler's response to him, also in Latin, has to do with legal procedure. The Graveneck text has *judica*, "give judgment," whereas the others have *indica*, "make your accusation." Since the word was addressed to the prosecutor, and since his next word was to conclude his case, the latter is the more likely meaning.

33. The Graveneck report speaks of one judge, the printed text of several, other records of twenty-four. Sattler spoke to them in the plural. Both may be correct, in that Joachim presided over a panel.

34. Only here does it become literally clear that Sattler challenges the authority of the court and refuses judicial process (cf. above note 13).

35. *Appellieren*: the legal term for appeal to a higher tribunal.

36. This sentence is only in the Graveneck report.

37. Graveneck: "But bore like the apostles all the mockery of his person."

38. That Sattler was or could have become a "lord" probably refers to his position, real or potential, as a prior in the monastery before his adhesion to Anabaptism.

39. Literally "to forge." Instead of being simply tied with the chains, the chains themselves were to be forged by a smith attaching him permanently to the wooden frame ("ladder") of the wagon, which then was to be thrown into fire.

40. Here the pamphlet text ends with the following words: "His brothers executed by the sword, the sisters drowned, his wife, after many pleas, exhortation, and threats, in great constancy, also drowned after a few days. Happened on the 21st day of May, 1527." The previous sentence in the text is still part of the verdict of the judges. But this last sentence in the printed text telescopes into a report of the execution itself. This is probably a result of careless editorial abbreviation, indicating that the text as printed is not the earliest redaction.

41. Again "smithed."

42. A prearranged symbol of Sattler's faithfulness to the end is also reported by Reublin. See text p. 78.

43. Literally "fell asleep"; the verb *entschlafen* is borrowed from the New Testament usage as a designation of death even when the manner of dying is violent.

44. The following text is the concluding portion of the letter ("nüwe zitung") written by Wilhelm Reublin to the Anabaptists of Switzerland. It was presumably copied by hand and circulated in several copies, one of which ultimately found its way to the Zürich Archives. It was written after July 17, 1527 (the date of the recantation which it

reports), presumably on the basis of firsthand reports. Reublin himself would hardly have been an eyewitness. The earlier portions of the report summarize the constitution of the body of judges and the trial procedure. We here reproduce only the conclusion.

45. We have referred before to the currency of the phrase "wedded sister" (*ehelich schwester*) as designation of a believing wife.

46. The sentence in parentheses (the parentheses are in the original) is unclear. What is the meaning of the "love" which caused him inner struggle?

In other contexts the term "love" could be used as designation of one's motivation for abandoning Anabaptism, namely out of consideration for the welfare of society. (J. H. Yoder, "Balthasar Hubmaier and the Beginnings of Swiss Anabaptism," *MQR* XXXIII (1959) p. 5; also H. Bullinger, "How to Deal with Anabaptists," *MQR* XXXIII (1959) pp. 88, 90, 95.) But the reference might also be to Sattler's pastoral concern for the churches, as testified to in his letter to Horb.

47. The reason for cutting off the tongue of a condemned person before his execution was to avoid the effect which this kind of last words could have on the onlookers. The most likely explanation for the anomaly of Sattler's speaking as here reported would be that these admonitions were addressed to the *Schultheiss* prior to the beginning of the torture, while Sattler was attached to the "ladder." The prior private conversation with the *Schultheiss*, to which allusion is made here, is not in the trial reports, unless we should identify it with the one "in a room" described by von Graveneck (p. 75).

48. The sack of gunpowder was intended by its exploding to hasten mercifully the death of the martyr.

49. Counter to the instructions of the court verdict Sattler was apparently tied with ropes rather than forged to the "ladder." His arms came free when the ropes had burned through.

50. The first scholar to reproduce this document in a collection of source materials, Johann Konrad Füsslin, commented thus on this collection of exceptional signs: "These are not miraculous signs, for one finds many such examples in history. Zwingli's heart could not be burned either. Still the people of Zürich did not make a miracle of it. The papists, however, considered it one, a sign of the spirit of error." *Beyträge zur Erläuteruug der kirchen-reformationgeschichte des Schweitzerlands* . . . (Band II) Zürich, 1741, p. 374. Füsslin, however, denies that there were letters in the sky, since to justify a revelation there would have had to be an interpretation, as in the case of Daniel in the Babylonian Court (Dan. 5).

51. The first named, Mathius Hiller, was from St. Gall, and had been taken captive at the same time as Sattler, perhaps having traveled with him from Schleitheim. The fact that Reublin names these four in a report to the Swiss churches might indicate that Schumacher, Lentzi, and Giger as well were from Switzerland. The names are Swiss.

52. This reference to "human grace" confirms the report of Valerius Anshelm (below) of the efforts of the countess to persuade her to recant.

53. The term "accepted" refers to the authorities' acceptance of the professed desire of the condemned Anabaptists to recant.

54. An addition by another hand at the end of this text reports "Wilhelm Reublin's wife is in prison in Horb with a one-and-one-half-year-old son, since the second week after Easter." This would mean that about May 1, two weeks before the other prisoners were moved from Binsdorf to Rottenburg, Reublin's wife had been moved back from Binsdorf to Horb, perhaps out of consideration for the youth of her child, which presumably exempted her from the trial proceedings.

55. Valerius Anshelm of Bern maintained an extensive chronicle of the events of his time. Largely limited to events in and around Bern, it reported more distant happenings only when they seemed especially significant. His acquaintance with the news

of Sattler's death can be explained only partly by the published accounts. Anshelm's wife was from Horb or Rottenburg and the family connections may well have contributed to his acquaintance with the reputation of Michael's wife. *Berner Chronik,* V, Bern, 1896, p. 185.

56. The bulk of this last paragraph confirms Reublin's report of the recantation of several of the Anabaptists and of their punishment. The last sentence is less clearly linked to the Sattler story, and may be derived from some other act of persecution.

V

The Capito Letters

Introduction

Wolfgang Capito was the most ecumenically open of the Reformers in Strasbourg. When the momentous choices had to be made, he stood with Martin Bucer for the maintenance of the state-supported pedobaptist church. Yet in willingness to converse with others and in ethical sensitivity he was closer to the dissenters. He had something to do with Strasbourg's remaining more tolerant than any other of the south German cities. This correspondence represents one of the few documents testifying to the existence of fraternal esteem across the growing divisions within the Reformation. It is a testimony to Capito's own exceptional breadth of charity, and also to Sattler's reputation among the Reformers.

The Text
The Capito Letters

A. *Letter to Bürgermeister and Council at Horb*, 31 May 1527[1]

May God the Father and our Lord Jesus Christ grant to you, honorable, wise lords, to understand His grace and mercy, so as not to collide with the Word of His kingdom at which all of the children of perdition take offense. Amen.

We[2] have heard that several persons have been taken captive and are in the hands of the Royal Majesty of Bohemia,[3] who had received the Word of God in a dangerous way and undertaken to believe in a particular manner and form,[4] of whom four have very recently been executed by the sword and the fifth, Michael by name, as their leader and instigator is said to have been condemned to death by a triple judgment, namely that in the city his tongue was cut out, second, that his body was torn with red hot tongs twice in the city and three times again at the gallows, thus tearing out his flesh, and third, that he was burned alive, all of which has taken place.

This Michael was known to us here in Strasbourg and did hold to some errors regarding the Word, which we sought faithfully to show him by Scripture. But since besides in addition to our faithful teaching and that of other preachers there may well be shortcomings among the people who claim to be Christian, a life found to be offensive,[5] it was for this reason, if I understand, that he took so little to heart what we basically[6] argued to clarify the truth. But he demonstrated at all times an excellent zeal for the honor of God and the church of Christ, which he desired to see righteous and honorable, free of vices, irreproachable, and to be by their righteous life a help to those who are without. This intention we never reprimanded but rather praised and encouraged. But the means he proposed and his articles[7] we rejected, in all friendliness toward him as a fellow member in Christ. This we did with fear and trembling as before the face of God, that we might not have been opposing hastily something that was truly of God, for the spirit of fear and of counsel teaches us thus to act.[8]

Now we were not in agreement with him as he wished to make Christians righteous by their acceptance of articles and an outward commitment.[9] This we thought to be the beginning of a new monasticism. We desired rather to help the believing life to progress by contemplation of the mercies of God, as Moses bases his exhortations to good works, on the reminder of divine favors and of the fatherly disciplining of the people by God (Deut. 8); which is the order[10] of salvation. Namely that we confess our sin and know that God has forgiven us the same through Christ, and that out of pure grace He desires to give us eternal life, of which we are assured by the Spirit of the children of God, which then gives birth to fear, yea, which penetrates us with fear, so that we become conscientious in all our action that we might not act against God. This is followed by wisdom, understanding, counsel, strength, and pure childlike reverence which remains eternally. But it can happen that the elect of God have this fear and desire from their hearts to serve God, but have not yet received the spirit of wisdom and do not really know that God looks only on the yielded heart,[11] rather think they will please Him with their works. Such persons are certainly saved and have a good zeal, but not with right knowledge. These are to be loved as brothers and fellow members, to be dealt with tenderly in their weakness, in their ignorance to be shown the truth with a mild spirit. This is what Paul calls accepting the brother who is weak in the faith,[12] which is what faith and love for the honor of God and brotherly love toward the neighbor demand of all of us. The more understanding one is, the more it behoves him to take care for the weak vessel and the ignorant brother. And to do this in true humility and yieldedness, so that we ourselves may not be tempted and please ourselves, who should be seeking only to please others for their betterment, since understanding is a gift of God and not of our own doing and we can become knowledgeable in the kingdom of God only by grace and not by our own force or our own skill. We owe this consideration to our enemies, who as Paul says persecute the church of God unknowingly; how much more do we owe it to those who are certainly members of Christ, who ask instruction of us. St. John writes: "If someone has this world's goods and sees his brother in need[13] and closes his heart to him, how remains the love of God in him" (1 Jn. 3)? There can be no love of God in one who neglects to help an erring one toward a right understanding.

Now it is reported that after the judgment Michael requested and desired that learned men be sent to him[14] and that what they could teach him out of Scripture he would gratefully accept and be willing nevertheless to accept the judgment that had been pronounced. He asked only, since he was proclaimed to be in error, that for God's sake they would correct his error. Whereupon it is reported that someone, who had already had more to do with the shedding of innocent blood, is supposed to have said, "The hangman will instruct you" or "The hangman will have to debate with you." If this is the case, it is fearful to hear: against it stands an awful judgment of God, that anyone could by judicial decision take the life of someone to whom according to God they are obligated to give fraternal instruction. God the Almighty gave the sword to Moses and with the sword he condemns only such trespass as concerns the outward and civil community. The lawgiver did not punish any inward offenses (Deut. 27)[15]; for the public blasphemy which the lawgiver punished with death also had to do with the public welfare. Michael and his following cannot be accused of such, for they are no blasphemers, as far as we can know anything of their nature. Unless you consider it to be blasphemy that the poor people have undertaken to avoid lascivious playing, drinking, gluttony, adultery, war, murder, gossip, living according to fleshly lusts, and to flee what is of the world and according to the flesh.

It is true that, if they believe baptism upon confession to be necessary for salvation, they are in error. And when they say that the government may not be Christian, that one should not swear any oath, or should not defend oneself against enemies under the government, they are also in error. For our Lord Christ is too high to be tied to water, and our salvation is much too powerful and certain, yea, God Himself is much too majestic, to be tied to one particular station or not to be able to accept someone from a certain station,[16] He who wills that all men might be saved, to whom nothing is contrary which is according to love, for love is the end of the law.[17] So in whatever station one can trust Christ and serve the neighbor this is not against Christ. Now government was to serve the community and to attenuate its disorder (Deut. 1).[18] Therefore it is not unchristian. This is the order, that there should be government, as a reward for good and as a menace for evil works. He who resists this order, resists God the Almighty. But when the kingdom of Christ will have come in its full force, what now is only fragmentary and among a few, then we shall all be immediately[19] directed and ruled by the righteous David, we will all be just, righteous, and yielded. Then there will be no room for the use of the sword, for the evil ones, whom it is to frighten, will have been killed by the spirit of the mouth of God and done away with and will be no more. On these points our dear brothers and strong confessors of the truth may have been in error and the remaining ones who are still in prison in your city may still be [in error], but in other points they are wonderful witnesses to the truth and vessels of honor, and these errors do not endanger their salvation. For the foundation stands fast: God knows those who are His own, whom He chose before the foundation of the world was laid.

These imprisoned people who are in your city are certainly of this number, for there is certainly within them the fear of God and it is because of their earnestness and zeal to further the glory of God that they have come into error. Their foundation is truly that we must hear Christ the Son of God and that he who believes in Him has eternal life. This foundation stands fast against the gates of hell. On it, however, they build wood, hay, and stubble, which the fire will take away, and they will be saved, but through fire (1 Cor. 3).[20] Thus with them it all depends finally on the first foundation, on Christ and the grace of God. Now woe to those who persecute Christ in these innocent people and who do not apply themselves all the more to correct their own shortcomings; for such do not only harass but in fact persecute outright the feeble flock of Christ, they who should be fathers and shepherds. Why do they not think that they have been established to provide temporal government and have no mandate to be the masters of faith or to quench the spirit of Christ in the hearts when even Moses, the man of God, governed only the external order, and this according to God? Whoever then wants to honor God with the sword, let him punish adultery, usury, murder, and other things which contradict the wholesome teaching of the gospel, the vices which these servants of God flee and avoid, as is evident and undeniable. Yea, it is frightful to hear that among Christian rulers there should be less mildness toward witnesses of Christ than there was among the stiff-necked Pharisees. These said, in their action toward Paul, we find nothing offensive on this man. If a spirit or an angel had spoken to him, we would not want to oppose God (Acts 23).[21] If the prisoners have acted contrary to civil law, for instance stolen, robbed, rebelled, or done something of the like, they do not concern us. But if their lives are innocent and they desire according to the order of love to honor God, even if they be somewhat mistaken, then their innocence and their lack of understanding cannot make them liable to bodily punishment. He who can should help them, for God commands, if a man finds his enemy's ass wandering, he should put him on the path.[22] He much more requires that we should help, guide, and lead our dear friends, brethren, comrades in the faith, fellow members in Christ, faithfully along the way of God.

So: for those who are still alive I plead and beg, for those hearts who are in prison with God and yet suffer no little affliction, that their faith has been proclaimed to be error and yet that there is no one who has disclosed their error to them with Scripture. Here it belongs to you, honorable wise lords, to apply every effort so that your brothers and fellow citizens may not be overrun and mistreated, through appropriate ways and means to bring to the light their innocence and their honorable life, to plead fervently for them that their error might not be punished with torture, but that in a friendly way they might be better taught where they are in error, although in the main points of the faith and its meanings they are not at all wrong, which at the last judgment all of the elect, yea, even the damned will have to testify to.[23]

And even if it might not be possible at once to convince them of all the secondary points, then one must take time until God gives grace; for one should not break a bruised reed or quench a glowing flax.[24] There are some sicknesses of the soul which cannot be healed at once like lightning with a single treatment. They are nevertheless confessors of the faith and of the honor of God and therefore children of God and they must speak as they believe. For what good would it be if out of fear they said, "we have been enlightened, we recognize our error," but in the heart they still held to their former thoughts? Faith is in the heart; the believers work to acquire a right understanding; otherwise a pretended righteousness is a double evil.

I have been sufficiently informed, dear friends, that you are no longer the judges,[25] but nevertheless you have been willing, out of civil friendship to help your accused fellow citizens in temporal things in an appropriate way, such as through a respectful report to the government, which is already so notorious, that it will not bother anyone for testifying to [the prisoners'] innocence, and would not hold it against you if you made all possible effort to getting such righteous persons free. I tell you it is true, what you do to these poor ones, that you have done to Christ, who suffers with them. And if by the speech of evil men the hearts of the authorities should be hardened, and it should please God that these captives should testify to the death of Christ with their own blood, you would have at least done your part and would be further obliged in all patience without contradiction to suffer and to accept what God would have, which is within the power of the heart of the princes. If it pleases Him He will turn them for the better and form in them another understanding. Otherwise in protecting [them] you would be fighting against God, even as on the other hand the persecution of the innocent fights against God to its own destruction. Authority is such a high and divine thing, that we can be obliged for conscience' sake even to suffer its injustice.

In sum: I commend your prisoners to you in the Lord; defend their innocence as comrades and at least try to see that according to their request they might be better instructed, for you are obligated before God to do that. If your brotherly testimony does not help, then commit them to God and to suffer imprisonment, until God, who does not keep His wrath eternally and who wills that each one carry his cross with patience and thus find rest in suffering and life in death, Himself redeems you[26] just as the Jews, who did not resist the king of Babylon, were less reprimanded than the others, who, against God's will, wanted to free themselves and defend themselves against the tyrants, may God enlighten the hearts of the overlords with a knowledge of Himself and His Son and may He increase our faith and give to all who for the sake of His honor are being tested in the truth, to be able to stand fast unto the end in all patience and yieldness. Amen.

Strasbourg, 31[27] May 1527. Wolfgang Capito and several Christian brothers[28] at Strasbourg.

B. Letter to the Prisoners at Horb[29]

Grace, peace, and strength from God the Father be with you dear brothers and sisters, that you might follow in the footprints of His Son our Lord, in all patience and yieldedness.[30] Amen.

All of us[31] who serve God in the same spirit through His Son Jesus Christ, mourn with you, suffer and bear your imprisonment and persecution in our flesh, being one with you in Christ and members of the one Head. But much more we rejoice in the inner man, who has insight into the judgments and counsels of God and recognizes that this testing is profitable for patience, wherein you experience your faith, which being thus tested by fire, is found to be much more precious than the gold which passes away.[32] Thus our flesh is in tribulation and mourning but the spirit is sovereignly exalted and rejoices with you. So good is God with His elect, that in all things He disposes for good out of His fatherly will.

He considers you worthy to believe in Him and to suffer for the sake of His name.[33] For you are not in prison for murder, theft, adultery, or other evil deeds, but rather as Christians,[34] although the poor people who are acting against you perhaps do not understand this. How should you then mourn and be ashamed rather than praising God for this matter, who is in this way beginning His judgment at the house of God with you,[35] refining you through fire and leading you up to a clear understanding and experience of His goodness.

But be attentive lest the enemy of your hearts precipitate you into impatience and give you to imagine that such persecution comes from men. The hairs of your head are counted by God, not one can fall to the earth without His will. He loves you heartily as His children and does everything for your welfare. So protect yourselves, that the enemy not seduce you toward an irreverent judgment and make you consider your persecutors, namely all men who have now forsaken you or are against you, as your enemies and members of the devil. For the elect Paul, a precious member of Christ, helped to stone and to kill Stephen and persecuted the church out of zeal for the honor of God, for the reprobate neither know nor acknowledge God.[36] So that it might be that those who, in their ignorance, now persecute you might be in good standing before God and might in time be sharers in our salvation. For the children of God will only be united at the revelation of the exalted Christ, who is still hidden from many. Therefore your duty is to bewail their blindness and pray for them and not at all to hate them as enemies, since God is acting through them. Above all, it is necessary that through powerful patience you convince your own hearts, that they might see that God is with you and that you do not manifest an unworthy attitude to anyone. Thus you stop the mouth of those who speak evil of you.[37] We hope also before God the Lord that you will constantly confess the precious blood of Christ, through which alone we are washed, which alone is to be praised, through which alone we are redeemed for life, for resurrection, and for the kingdom of God, through which we recognize the sovereign goodness and grace of God who is bound to no one, but who imparts saving faith in Christ Jesus, which itself alone constitutes eternal life, to whom, how and when He will. Under the cross this understanding will become more and more clear and will grow.

This without any further supplement should be your confession. Out of it other points can be derived and may well instruct you concerning baptism and the Lord's Supper and how baptism as a sign of dying to self in Christ is only genuinely executed when we die in the Lord. Which is an external thing and subject to love[38] which accepts and orders it for godly betterment as order requires and permits at each time.

Further, dear brothers, as long as there are evil deeds, government is ordained for a menace to the evil and a reward to good works and can be administered in love.[39] Therefore a Christian can be an overlord and can serve God in his command. But not everyone is apt for such. Therefore one can say for himself that he does not know how he could be at the same time a Christian and an overlord, yet not judge other persons who perhaps are more gifted. For God's grace is richer and broader than that it should exclude a particular station. There are manifold gifts,[40] some rule through the same spirit, etc.[41] Therefore I obey my temporal government as I obey God the Lord and consider that the divine order for our time is thus. And what it commands me, whether it be to take weapons, to protect the fatherland, and otherwise, I do with a good conscience, as the Jews under the commandment of Hezekiah their king resisted the king of Babylon and did right therein.[42] For it is the same God who through Christ has given us salvation, who has a certain order and means of dealing with all the elect, which Christ did not change but rather fulfilled, for the Son cannot be against the Father. This order is that according to His election He places His seed in the heart of the elect, whereby they are brought to yieldedness and to the fear of

God which moves the spirit of the children of God. There-after follows confidence in the promise of God, which pre-eminently pointed to Christ and has been fulfilled, namely that the sin of the world has been laid upon Him and that eternal life consists in such knowledge of God and of Christ as He imparts to all the elect. This is the order of salva-tion, toward which God in every time through appropriate external means furthers those who always press toward faith and love, and may externally change but internally seen is an immutable order.[43]

Neither do I complain of the oath, which I perform out of obedience and for the welfare of my neighbor, unselfishly. For I know that I should swear in His name and should thereby confess Him: for to swear correctly is to keep the command of God and to honor Him (Ex. 20 [7]; Deut. 10 [20]; Jer. 4 [2]), according to all Scripture.[44] But further according to the exposition of Christ I apply myself that my word "yea" should be "yea" and my "nay nay;" what is beyond this is of the evil one and is wrong. And as far as I am concerned I need no swearing or no testimony before God; but in order to honor God I serve the neighbor thereby. This is the understanding of the Spirit of God, which I hold before God and all the world certainly and assuredly.

But if God does not yet teach you this, then remain in the confessing of the blood of Christ and request instruction on the other points, so that your persecutors might persecute in you Christ alone and nothing else. And therein do you please God. For he who has the most exalted Christ in the heart, he does not let himself be led astray by outward things but uses the same for the welfare of the neighbor according to the measure of faith and does his work in the fear of God, out of constraining love, voluntarily and without coercion.

The whole of my admonition is that your duty is only, as Peter says,[45] to give the reason for your hope and to con-fess it freely, which consists alone therein, that we are purified from sin through the sprinkling of the blood of Christ, and it includes no other points. Therefore what you are unsure of, you can with yielded speech ask for instruction for God's sake, and speak this confession in all yieldedness as before God the Lord. For your judges in this are servants of God and His instruments to do His will and command for the furthering of the salvation of your souls and the praise and honor of God. Believe and meditate on this fervently to strengthen your patience. With you we will fervently call upon God for help and grace and we beg of you that you would also pray God for us for more faith and knowledge of Him that He would use us all for His glory. Amen.

Strasbourg;

A faithful brother and companion in your hope in the Lord, whose name God knows.[46]

To my dear brothers and sisters who are now testifying with their own bodies to Christ the crucified One, by their imprisonment and suffering at Horb.

Notes

1. Krebs/Rott I, No. 83, pp. 80 ff.

2. Capito's first draft was begun in the singular; then rewritten to indicate the support of several others.

3. Ferdinand of Austria had just in the last months become King of Bohemia.

4. A delicate way of alluding to Anabaptism without using a precise name.

5. I.e., at which Sattler took offense. Capito explains Sattler's unwillingness to accept his arguments as partly attributable to the fact that the quality of life of the "Christians" at Strasbourg belied the faithfulness of the preachers.

6. "Gründlich" in modern usage would probably be rendered "thoroughly"; but here Capito is rather claiming that his and Bucer's arguments went solidly to the bottom of things.

7. "Articles" may mean the outline of issues referred to by Sattler (above p. 21f).

8. Is. 11:2. It is not clear whether the allusion to the guidance of the Spirit is meant to explain why Capito and his colleagues were mild against Sattler, or why they opposed him. As distinct from their treatment of Denck, Capito testifies that in opposing Sattler the Reformers were uneasy, sensing some validity in his witness.

9. The first draft here had "confession"; Capito then changed it to a term carrying a flavor of forced or external obligation. Thus part of what Sattler called for was that Christians should commit themselves visibly to a particular discipline. The "agreed points" or "articles" may well be those of note 7 above, or a shorter list of issues like the seven of Schleitheim, or perhaps just the idea of an explicit baptismal covenant.

10. "Order" here means not only "the way God ordains" but also "proper sequence." Proper behavior follows from the message of grace; therefore a prescribed behavior must not be a prerequisite to church membership.

11. The use of "yielded" here is significant; cf. p. 23, art. 15. It is Capito, not Sattler as Bossert had said, who understands "yieldedness" here in a quietistic way. Yet a few lines later it again will have a social and ethical dimension.

12. Rom. 14:1.

13. The text of 1 Jn. 3:17 is clearly shown by the context to have to do with this world's goods. Capito's reading, however, " . . . und sihet in sym bruder mangel. . . ," is more easily understood as "if you see your brother has something wrong with him." Thus he takes the text as an admonition, parallel to Gal. 6:1 f., to patient acceptance of the ignorant and spiritually weak, whom one seeks patiently to instruct. Capito begins this paragraph as a criticism of Sattler's impatience in wanting to impose Christian maturity by "points and articles," but skillfully generalizes and shifts focus so that by the end he is on the same grounds reprimanding Sattler's judges for not respecting his willingness to be taught.

14. According to our reports of the trial of Sattler (cf. above pp. 73), his challenge to his judges to let him be shown his error by theologians was at the beginning of the trial, not after the judgment. We, however, noted an unclarity in the sources as to the time of a separate meeting with the *Schultheiss.*

15. Deut. 27:15 ff.

16. Protestantism began its criticism of clericalism by arguing that no one particular station is privileged ("God is too majestic to be bound to our station"); now the same argument is turned in the opposite direction to argue that no particular station in life, namely that of government, is especially *un*acceptable to God. Thus the same argument which worked against clericalism works in favor of the maintenance of the Christian magistracy.

17. This is the text which Sattler in his letter to Capito and Bucer had identified as 1 Tim. 1:5; it could also be Rom. 13:10.

18. Deut. 1:13 recounts the naming of the heads of tribes by Moses. Capito takes this (rather than Gen. 9) as the institution of government within salvation history.

19. I.e., without any means, without intervening instruments between the Messiah and His subjects.

20. 3:12 f.

21. 23:9.

22. Ex. 23:4.

23. It is not sure to what even the damned will have to testify; is it the innocence of the Anabaptists or is it the main points of the faith? The latter is more likely.

24. Is. 42:3.

25. The government at Horb first wanted to retain the prisoners, perhaps with a view to being more merciful, but jurisdiction was taken away from them by the Austrian government. His acknowledgment of this change means that Capito is not so much pleading with the judges for mercy as he is supporting similar concerns which he thinks may also be present in Horb.

26. Capito seems to have shifted the addressees of his letter: the latter part of this sentence would seem to be addressed to the prisoners. If this is not a mental lapse, it is a testimony to the degree of moral solidarity which Capito presupposes (cf. note 25) between the authorities or the population at Horb and the prisoners. If the Horb council was not pro-Anabaptist, it may at least very well have been anti-Austrian and slow to persecute.

27. The draft was first dated 28th of May. Some time elapsed while Capito showed it to the others in whose name it was written. Then their names were removed; perhaps because they were either more or less critical of Sattler than Capito had been in the draft.

28. The draft first read, "Capito, Mathias Zell, and the other servants of the Word and preachers."

29. Krebs-Rott, No. 84, 87 ff. The document is undated but may be assumed to be of the same date as the preceding one. They are written in the same hand.

30. Cf. note 11 above.

31. "All of us" presumably means the same body of preachers at Strasbourg who wrote the preceding letter; Capito is thus not writing only for himself.

32. 1 Pet. 1:7.

33. Phil. 1:29.

34. 1 Pet. 4:15 f.

35. 1 Pet. 4:17.

36. This is one of the early testimonies to the conception of predestination which later came to be considered typical of the Calvinistic Reformation. If Saul, the persecutor, was to become Paul the Apostle, he was already elect when he was persecuting the church, even though it was impossible for the Christians whom he was pursuing to recognize this.

37. 1 Pet. 2:15.

38. For the meaning of the concept of love in Reformed thought, especially as a source of guidance in external matters and as an alternative to the instructions of Scripture, cf. above p. 26, note 47.

39. 1 Pet. 2:14.

40. 1 Cor. 12:4.

41. That "government" is one of the gifts of the Spirit can be read in 1 Cor. 12: 28, which Capito probably telescopes in his mind with the beginning of the same chapter.

42. 2 Chron. 32.

43. Here is one of the early Reformed statements of the unity of Old and New Testament, differing only in external forms, internally immutable. This equation of Old and New Testament later came to be a universal axiom of the Reformation response to Anabaptist criticism. Cf. Bullinger, *loc. cit.* (Note 38), pp. 84-86.

44. Only at this point does Capito himself indicate the texts to which he refers: the other Scripture allusions are identified by the editors.

45. 1 Pet. 3:15.

46. This text is unsigned. The reason for anonymity might be that Capito feared the consequences for Strasbourg if his moral support to the prisoners at Horb would become public knowledge. Perhaps he felt the letter was less likely to be confiscated if anonymous; or he might even have thought that Anabaptists would be more likely to read it if it did not have his name attached.

VI

On Divorce

Introduction

Already in the early prints of the *Seven Articles* and the martyrdom account, one of the tracts in our collection was also printed, namely this one on divorce. The process of agglomeration continued, forming a progressively larger collection of materials which by the middle of the century was substantially similar to our present collection,[1] except for the Strasbourg letters and "How Scripture. . . ." Even the hymn, "When Christ with His Teaching True" was included in a seventeenth-century reprinting of the collection.

The authorship of Sattler for these materials is relatively likely only for the tract on divorce, and even here the only grounds is its inclusion in the 1533 pamphlet, a consideration which must be weighed against the signature initials "M.L."[2] By 1626 when Peter Jansz Twisck compiled the Mennonite martyrology *Historie van de Vrome Getuygen Jesus Christi*, Sattler's authorship for the entire collection was taken for granted, but only on the circumstantial grounds of the repeated reprinting of the *SB* volume as a unit.[3] Since the *SB* ends with a text directly attributed to Melchior Rinck, there is no strong presumption for Sattler's authorship, except such as may be established from consideration of the content. The title we have chosen for the present collection, "The Legacy of Michael Sattler," reflects the fact that, despite some possible serious doubts about the authorship of some of the texts, they nonetheless all spring from the movement of which Sattler was a major architect and may worthily serve as to document the character of his movement.

It is difficult for the modern reader to grasp how strategic in the spreading of the Reformation, especially of Anabaptism, was the circulation of tracts like these. Populations newly literate, with limited reading material available, excited by the sense of impending radical change which pervaded German-speaking Europe in the 1520s, seized upon such fragments of literary witness with avidity. Their simplicity was adapted to the layman's demand for a faith in the words of the people; colporting tracts was a mode of missionary witness accessible even to those barely able to read for themselves. Many of them, like Balthasar Hubmaier's classic work on believers' baptism,[4] Conrad Grebel's notes on baptism,[5] or Sattler's(?) "How Scripture Should Be Discerningly Exposited," were not merely written sermons but study outlines for repeated use.

It is no accident that (after the questions of the sword and the oath dealt with at Schleitheim), divorce was the first ethical question needing close attention among Anabaptists. The actual position which Sattler (if it is he) takes here is not significantly different from that of other Protestants;[6] but the context of persecution, itineration, and exile gave it quite a different meaning, by making it a very current thing that man and wife could be separated because of the faith of one of them.

Comment on the theological content is limited here to such annotation as is demanded by unclear allusions or technical terms. Further evaluation of the significance of these texts is contributed by Robert Friedmann.[7] J. C. Wenger provides brief helpful commentary alongside each of his translations.

The Text
On Divorce[8]

From the words of Christ, Mt. 5 and 19; Mk. 10; Lk. 16:

The Pharisees tempted Jesus in order to trap Him, saying: "Is it right, that a man divorce his wife for just any small reason?" To whom Jesus holds forth the ordinance of His Father, saying: "Have you never read Gen. 1 and 2,[9] that he who in the beginning created man, provided that there should be one man and one wife, and said, 'therefore shall man forsake father and mother and cleave to his wife, and the two become one flesh.' So now they are not two, but one flesh, and what God has united, man shall not divide."

Still the tempters were not satisfied and they cite[10] Moses, Deut. 24: that Moses permitted one to divorce for any displeasure, whom Christ answers: "Moses permitted it because of the hardness of your hearts, but from the beginning it was not so. But I say to you: he who divorces, unless it be for fornication, and takes another, he commits adultery, and he who takes the divorced wife, also commits adultery."

Here (like Christ) we do not permit that one divorce his wife, unless it be for fornication, i.e., because of adultery. For when Christ says, "but I say to you . . ." as He also does often in Mt. 5, He abrogates the law, insofar as it is conceived literally[11] and not spiritually, Eph. 2,[12] as He is also the perfecting of the law, Rom. 10.[13] Therefore He is the mediator of a better Testament, which is founded upon better promises, Heb. 8.[14] Therefore He abrogates the former divorcing, (Deut. 24) and no longer makes concessions to hardness of heart, but rather renews the ordinance[15] of His Father, Gen. 1 and 2, saying: "From the beginning it was not so." Since then God so created, that there should be one husband and one wife, and what God has united, that let man not separate.

Therefore any minor cause — anger, which is hardness of heart; displeasure, contrariety, faith or unbelief — may not separate, but only fornication. He who divorces without fornication, the only reason, and remarries, commits adultery; and he who takes a divorced woman causes her to commit adultery; for Christ says, "These two are one flesh." But he who cleaves to a harlot, as Paul says, 1 Cor. 6,[16] sins against his own body and is one flesh with the harlot. Thus he is by this act separated from his own flesh, in that he has attached himself to the alien flesh of the prostitute, and thus the marriage is broken; for they are no longer one flesh, since the fornicator has become one flesh with the harlot. The one who finds herself thereby divorced may[17] now marry, whom she will, only let it be in the Lord,[18] that is, let her not marry[19] an apostate person, godless, but a believer, who holds to God, lest the unbelieving one seduce her away from God. Ex. 7.[20]

But then Paul writes, 1 Cor. 7[21]: "When the unbeliever does not desire to live with the believer, and despairs, let him depart, a sister or brother is not captive in such a case, for God called us in peace." This does not weaken or contradict the Word of Christ: else Paul would be speaking according to Moses, if hardness of heart, or unbelief, could separate. Then Paul would be scattering, as Christ says: "He who does not gather with me scatters,"[22] and that could not edify the body of Christ. But Paul is to be understood in this chapter, as he then also says, "We have the mind of Christ" and "I also believe I have the Spirit of God."

There are many reasons for unbelievers to give in favor of divorce, one thus and another otherwise. Sometimes also unbelief hates and persecutes faith in its works. As Christ testifies: "those of your household will be your enemies";[23] thus out of hostility and anger the believer will be pressed and driven out by the unbeliever, but that is still no divorce before God, for they are still one flesh, in that neither has forsaken his flesh to cleave to the alien flesh of a harlot, and become one flesh with the harlot, since fornication alone divorces. He who cleaves to the Lord is one spirit with Him, 1 Cor. 6, and flesh of His flesh and bone of His bones, Eph. 5: "which is a great mystery, I speak of Christ and his church"; for we are also a bride and spouse of Christ, 2 Cor. 11; Hos. 2; Apoc. 19, wedded to Him in faith. We leave father and mother, wife and children, fields and meadows, also our own life, Mt. 10; 19; Lk. 14, cleave to Him and are with Him one spirit. If then it comes to that, that we must forsake one or the other bride and spouse and stick with the other, having to choose either to do wrong, to forsake the love and communion of God and faith, and to cleave more to the fleshly spouse with whom we are one flesh, than to the spiritual spouse Christ;[24] now there is a combat, and it will be seen who loves more his wife, husband and child, fields and meadows. And now it becomes manifest, who are the elect of God, as 4 Esdras 16 speaks,[25] who forsake all, and follow after Christ under the cross daily.[26]

And then a brother or sister in such cases is not captive. Marriage is truly a bond and makes it obligatory as Paul says, that one not be master of one's own body, but the other,[27] and neither may turn away from the other. And yet it is not so great before God,[28] that for the sake of the bond of marriage the believer must do wrong, love and obey the husband more than God,[29] in order to be able to remain one flesh with the unbeliever. Rather the spiritual obligation and marriage with Christ and faith, love, and obedience to God take priority, so that no creature should separate us from God and from the love of Christ. Rom. 8.[30] Thus one should forsake rather the fleshly than the spiritual, and not salve one's conscience with the marriage bond, by honoring more the fleshly duty and obligation than the spiritual, as stands written: "Who loves father, mother, wife and child, is not worthy of me, yea, even he who cannot forsake all and hate even his own life, renouncing all that he has." Luke 14.[31]

Thus you now hear on the ground of the Word of God, that hardness of heart and unbelief do not divorce, but only fornication, and as long as no alienation occurs with another flesh, they are still one flesh. Further: if a man or woman, separated without fornication, i.e., without adultery, takes another woman or another man,[32] we hold that to be fornication and not members of the body of Christ.[33] And he who takes the divorced one, him also we hold to be a fornicator according to the words of Christ. He who divorces further and does not fall in line with the words of Christ, scatters, and knows nothing;[34] him we would avoid according to the words of Christ, as an apostate who condemns himself. Tit. 3.[35]

I speak as with those who have understanding; judge what I say. May God give us understanding and wisdom from above in all things, unto the knowledge of Him and unto His praise, Amen.

Br. M. L.[36]

1533[37]

Notes

1. The divorce tract is in the early pamphlet (see p. 13, text B — Clemen-Köhler, *op. cit.*, II, p. 333). For the other items our collection follows the oldest extant *Sammelband* (cf. above p. 13). In *SB* the tract on satisfaction comes before that on divorce.

2. Cf. below note 36.

3. There are also Hutterian manuscript codices in which this same body of material appears together, but since the earliest is from late in the century (cf. R. Friedmann, *MQR*, XVI, 1942, pp. 88 f.), it does not represent an independent text.

4. "Von dem christlichen Tauf der Gläubigen," in Westin and Bergsten, pp. 116 ff.

5. Cf. Heinold Fast, "Hans Krusis Büchlein" in C. J. Dyck, ed., *op. cit.*, p. 43.

6. The position taken was so similar to that of other Reformation writers that Walter Köhler even thought this text was a collection of extracts from Martin Luther. Still the positions are not identical; the novelty of the present text's position is that it deals with families divided by the issue of faith. This could not apply in the same way within a *Volkskirche*. But neither does it allow that the family be broken by the faith issue, as *ME*, II, 74 f., would give one to understand. It provides for a separation where the unbelieving partner, or banishment, causes it, but not for remarriage as long as the other partner does not first remarry.

7. *Loc. cit.* (note 3).

8. First translated by John C. Wenger in the *MQR*, XXI, April 1947, pp. 114 ff. The Wenger translation is based upon the late 16th- or early 17th-century *Sammelband* referred to here as *SB*. The present translation is based on the 1533 pamphlet as produced by Köhler (above p. 13). Wenger has suggested that the *SB* original might be based on a separate German original text using a dialect from some region farther north than that represented by the *Flugschriften* text. The language differences would, however, seem rather to indicate the effect of the passage of time and editorial correction, rather than a separate linguistic tradition represented by other original texts. *SB* bears other marks of editorial polishing, such as the filling in of more biblical references and the balancing out of incomplete thoughts (e.g. 29 below).

9. The *SB* text adds a reference to Mal. 2. In general, the later *SB* text adds additional scriptural references, another evidence of its being a later edition.

10. There is a confusion of tenses throughout in the narrative paragraphs. This is grammatically understandable as a way to make the narrative contemporary. Some of this confusion is smoothed out in the *SB* text.

11. Wenger suggests "legalist" as a rendering for "literal."

12. 2:15.

13. 10:4.

14. 8:6.

15. *Ordnung*, the word translated "ordinance," is a verbal noun which still retains something of its verbal ring. The reference to Genesis 1 and 2 alludes not to a particular law thought of as having been promulgated by God as legislator, but rather to the action of God, the "ordering," seen as bringing into being an arrangement, the monogamous union of Adam and Eve, which is revelatory of His will. Cf. its use to speak of the "sword" of government, above pp. 39, 40. See also p. 52, notes 73f.

16. 6:16 and 18.

17. The writer is obviously thinking of the wife as being the one cast off. Wenger is certainly correct in suggesting in a footnote that, as far as the thought is concerned which underlies the tract, the same logic would apply as well to a husband whose marriage is broken by the infidelity of his wife. The thought is thus that since a given marriage partner can only be part of "one flesh" with one spouse at a time, the active infidelity itself constitutes a second unity and thereby *ipso facto* constitutes the revocation of the former bonds. Thus the former spouse is automatically but innocently divorced.

18. Here the *SB* text adds a reference to 1 Cor. 7:39, the original reference of which was to a widow.

19. Again it is assumed that the party who may remarry is the wife of an unfaithful husband. The case of the husband of an unfaithful wife is not dealt with.

20. Ex. 7:1 ff., *SB* adds Deut. 7.

21. 7:15. As Wenger comments, *scheiden* here refers to a separation of domicile and not such divorce as would permit the "innocent partner" freely to marry. The linguistic distinction between separation and divorce does not exist in the German, but it is just this distinction which our author is interested in making. He means to draw the line between the separation which is permitted in 1 Cor. 7:15 and that which is forbidden in Mt. 19. The problem was created for him by the use of *scheiden* in both cases. In the Greek the terms *apolusai* and *choristhenai* differ, in a way parallel to his argument.

22. Mt. 12:30.

23. Mt. 10:36.

24. The "either" is left dangling; the sentence is never completed with an "or."

25. Chapter 16 of *2 Esdras* (4 Esdras in medieval reckoning) is the conclusion of the book. The reference there to "my elect" climaxes a prophecy of warning addressed to the "servants of the Lord," 16:35 ff., after the earlier part of the chapter had addressed a prophecy of woe to Babylon, Asia, Egypt, and Syria (1-34): "Then the tested quality of my elect shall be manifest, as gold that is tested by fire. 'Hear, my elect,' says the Lord, 'Behold, the days of tribulation are at hand, and I will deliver you from them. Do not fear or doubt, for God is your guide.' "

26. This is the only paragraph break within the original text.

27. I.e., the "other," one's spouse, is master of one's body. 1 Cor. 7:14.

28. Wenger paraphrases correctly, "Yet the obligation is not so strong in God's sight. . . ."

29. The *SB* text completes here with the complementary "the man rendering greater obedience to his wife."

30. V. 35.

31. The quotation is a conflation of Lk. 14:26 and Mt. 10:37. The sequence "father and mother, wife and child, and all that he has" is most like Luke; yet "is not worthy of me" is from Matthew.

32. Here for the first time the writer balances both possibilities. The two parties

are separated (by the faith of one of them) but neither has yet been sexually unfaithful until the remarriage, which thereby itself constitutes adultery.

33. Here the phrase "members of the body" must be distinguished from "one flesh." The point here is that such persons are not (Anabaptist) Christians, not that they are not married.

34. This sentence is not redundant but rather, as the allusion to Mt. 12:30 indicates, a reference to teaching. "He who divorces further" does not mean a man who leaves his wife again, or who leaves his second wife; but rather any teacher who authorizes divorce beyond the case where the other partner has already been unfaithful.

35. Tit. 3:11 refers to one who is factious in controversies over the law. "To avoid," *(meiden)* as Wenger points out, does not prescribe a particular disciplinary procedure, as it does in later Mennonite usage.

36. Walter Köhler conjectured wrongly that the initials refer to Martin Luther and that his text is a series of extracts from a longer Luther work. That it might be a misprint for M(ichael) S(attler) has been suggested by Cramer (*BRN*, V, p. 597). If the initials are correct, the only prominent figure bearing such a name would be Martin Linck, also called Weniger (*ME*, III, p. 350) of Schaffhausen, a major spokesman of the movement in the early 1530s. By the time of his active ministry Anabaptism was widespread all over northern Switzerland, with banishment a frequent form of punishment. Thus the problem of the status of marriages broken by exile, i.e., by the unbelief of one partner and the banishment of the other, was a real one, as would hardly yet have been the case in 1526-27. Linck/Weniger was a leading Anabaptist participant in the Zofingen Gespräch of 1532; J. C. Wenger translated his *apologia* in *MQR*, XXII, 1948, p. 180.

37. This date may refer to either the writing of the tract or the date of the printing. In either case it fixes the *terminus a quo* for the printing of pamphlet B (cf. above p. 13) and probably argues for the priority of pamphlet A.

VII

On the
Satisfaction of Christ[1]

The Text

That Paul says to the Romans in the third chapter, "They are all together sinners and fall short of the praise which God should have from them, and are justified without merit, by his grace, through the redemption worked by Christ, whom God set forth as a mercy seat, through faith in his blood, so that he might demonstrate the righteousness which is valid before God in that he forgives the sins which had been committed before, under divine patience, which suffered, etc."[2] Item, that he says: "Of which you are also in Christ Jesus, who has been made by God wisdom, righteousness, sanctification and redemption for us, etc."[3] Item, that John the Baptist says (Jn. 1), "Behold, that is the Lamb of God, which takes upon itself the sin of the world." Item, that John says (1 Jn. 2), "And he is our reconciliation for our sin." Item, that Peter says (1 Pet. 2), "Who himself sacrificed for our sins in his body upon the tree so that we might be without sin." Item, that the prophet also says (Is. 53), "We are healed by his stripes." Item (Is. 9), "A child is born to us, a child is given, etc."

Such texts (I say) and other similar ones the scribes[4] explain in such a way as if man could be saved by Christ whether he does the works of faith or not. If that were so, why then does Paul say (Rom. 2), "God will give to each one according to his works, namely eternal life to those who seek after glory, praise and immortality with perseverance in good works, but to the contentious and those who are not obedient to the truth, but rather obey iniquity, shall come disfavor and wrath, tribulation and anxiety upon all the souls of men who do evil"? Further, he says (Rom. 2), "Not they who hear the law are righteous but they that do the law." Item, Paul says (Rom. 3), that he does not abolish the law through faith but establishes it. Item, he says (Rom. 8), "Now there is nothing to condemn those who are in Christ Jesus, who do not walk according to the flesh but according to the Spirit. For what was impossible to the law (since it had been weakened by the flesh) that God did, and sent his Son in the form of sinful flesh, and through sin condemned sin in the flesh, so that the righteousness which the law demands might be fulfilled in us, who now walk not according to the flesh but according to the Spirit." Item, "If you live according to the flesh you must die." Item, Gal. 5: "In Christ Jesus neither circumcision nor uncircumcision counts, but a faith which is active in love." Item, 1 Cor. 13: "If I had all faith, so that I could move mountains, but have not love, then I am nothing." Item, Eph. 5: "For you know that no adulterer, fornicator, or covetous man, that is, idolater, has any inheritance in the kingdom of Christ and of God. Let no one deceive you with vain words." Eph. 6: "Since you know that everyone will receive from the Lord what good he has done." Item, 2 Cor. 5: "For we must all appear before the judgment seat of Christ, so that each one might receive according to what he did with his body, whether good or evil." Likewise Peter (1 Pet. 1), "And since you call on the Father who judges all without any respect of persons, each according to his works, therefore complete the time of your pilgrimage with fear." Item, 2 Pet. 1: "And therefore bring forth, with the greatest diligence, from your faith virtue, from virtue knowledge, from knowledge temperance, from temperance patience, from patience godliness, from godliness brotherly love, out of brotherly love for all; for if such are abundant among you, they will not let you be lazy or inactive in the knowledge of our Lord Jesus Christ. He, however, who has not such, is blind and gropes." Item, John says (1 Jn. 1), "If we wish to say we have fellowship with him and walk in the darkness, we are lying and not doing the truth." Item, 1 Jn. 2: "Hereby we know that we have known him, as we keep his commandments. He who says he knows him and does not keep his commandment is a liar. . . . He who says he is in the light and hates his brother is in darkness." Item, 1 Jn. 3: "Children, let no one deceive you. He who does right is righteous as he is righteous; he, however, who commits sin is of the devil." Item, "He who is born of God no longer sins, for his seed remains in him and he cannot sin, for he is born of God." To say nothing of what Christ Himself says (Mt. 4): "Better yourselves,[5] for the kingdom of heaven has come near." He speaks to Peter and others, "Follow me." Item, Mt. 5: "Let your light shine before people that they may see your good works and praise your Father in heaven." Item, "You should not think that I have come to do away with the law and the prophets. I have not come to do away with but to fulfill." Item, Mt. 7: "Therefore he who hears this discourse of mine and does it, him I compare to a prudent man who built his house upon a rock. When then a sudden rain fell and floods came, the winds blew and pressed upon the house, yet it did not fall; for it was founded upon a rock. And he who hears this discourse of mine and does it not, he is like a foolish man who built his house upon sand." Item, Mt. 10: "He who confesses me before men, him I will confess before my Father in heaven." Item, "He who loves father or mother more than me is not worthy of me, and he who loves son or daughter more than me is not worthy of me." And what He says of the good seed which falls into the good earth, Mt. 13. Item, Mt. 16: Mk. 8; Lk. 9: "If someone desires to follow me, let him deny himself and take up his cross and follow me, for he who would preserve his life shall lose it, but he who renounces his life for my sake will find it." Item, Mt. 18: "For it shall come to pass that the Son of man will come in the glory of his Father with his angels and that he will reward each one according to his works." Item, Lk. 10: Christ says to the scribe that he should love

God from his whole heart and his neighbor like himself and thus he will live. Item, Lk. 13: "Strive to go in through the narrow gate." Item, Lk. 14: "If someone comes to me and does not hate his father, mother, wife, children, brethren, sisters, and even his own life, he cannot be my disciple. And he who does not carry his cross and follow after me cannot be my disciple." Item, Jn. 13: "I have given you an example that you do as I have done to you." Item, "If you know this, blessed are you if you do it." Item, "I give you a new commandment, that you love one another, as I have loved you. Thereby everyone shall know that you are my disciples, because you have love for another."

Further,[6] if Christ suffered thus for us (He who had no place to lay His head, Mt. 8) even if we never, through faith in Him, renounce the seeming ownership[7] of the creatures and ourselves and never suffer for His sake, why then does He say (Mt. 19) to the young man who asked Him how he should be saved, "If you would be perfect, go and sell what you have and give it to the poor, thus you will have treasure in heaven, and come, and follow after me"? Why does He say it is easier that a camel should go through the eye of a needle than for a rich man to enter the kingdom of God? And why does He say to Peter and Andrew in Lk. 5 (as we saw above), "Follow me"? Or to Matthew, "Follow me"? Does Zacchaeus not say (Lk. 19), after he had recognized and accepted the poor man Jesus, "Behold, I give half of my goods to the poor people, and if I have deceived someone that I restore fourfold"? Unless Jesus was lying when He said (Mt. 6) that we cannot serve God and mammon, and unless it were not true what Luke says (Acts 2), of the faithful Christian congregation which was then at Jerusalem, "But the faithful were in one assembly and held all things in common." Yea, even the articles of the Christian faith[8] would be false, which say, "the fellowship of the saints." Item, why does He then say (Mk. 8), "He who would follow me, let him deny himself, take up his cross and follow me"? Item, "He who would preserve his life shall lose it." Item, why does He say, Mt. 5, "Blessed are they who suffer persecution for righteousness' sake"? Item, "Blessed are you when men revile and persecute you and speak all manner of evil against you, falsely, for my sake." Item, Mt. 10; Jn. 15: "The disciple is not above his master, nor the servant above his lord; it is enough for the disciple to be as his master and the servant as his lord." Item, Jn. 16: "They will excommunicate you. The time is coming when whoever kills you will believe he is doing God a service." Item, "Verily, verily, I say to you, you shall weep and howl but the world will rejoice, etc. . . ." But does not also Peter say (1 Pet. 2), "For to this are you called, since Christ also suffered for us, and left us an example, that you should follow after in his footsteps"?[9] Yea, truly if Christ thus worked atonement[10] with the suffering He underwent in Jerusalem, so that nothing more is lacking in His suffering, why then does Paul say (Col. 1), "Now I rejoice in my suffering which I suffer for you, and fill out in my body what was lacking in the afflictions of Christ"? Item, 2 Cor. 1: "As we have tribulation or consolation, it is for your good." Item, Eph. 3: "Therefore I Paul, prisoner of Jesus Christ for you Gentiles." Item, Phil. 2: "And if I should be offered up as a sacrifice and worship[11] of your faith, I am glad and rejoice with you."

Just as if Christ had not established the Lord's Supper primarily because they must suffer, just like their head Christ, and through death enter into glory, yea, that their death would not be their own but the Lord's[12] and that they should also be resurrected just like the head. And where would the dear prophets and apostles be left, yea, also Christ Himself, who prophesied for so many years of the great suffering of the friends of God in this time,[13] if the members of Christ would not need to suffer just like the head?

Does not Peter say (1 Pet. 5), "Humiliate yourselves under the mighty hand of God, that he might exalt you at the right time. Cast all your care on him, for he cares for you. Be sober, watch, for your adversary the slanderer goes about like a roaring lion, seeking whether he might devour someone. Resist him, strengthened by faith, because you know that through your brotherhood, which is in the world, the same suffering is being perfected."

Therefore Paul says (Rom. 3), "That they who are justified through Christ, are made righteous without any merit, or without the works of the law." He does not mean that a man can be saved without the works of faith (since now Christ and the apostles require the same), but rather without such works which are accomplished outside of faith and the love of God, such as circumcision and the like were, which the Jews did in order that they might thereby be justified. For this reason Paul and Christ as well, whenever they give to works the name of "righteousness," do it because they are not the work of man, but of God and Christ (through whose power a man does such works) and do not happen because through them man achieves something as his own, but rather because God through them wishes to give to man something of His own.

And what should then a mercy seat be, if not that God thereby manifests His will among His own? But why should God manifest His will, if He did not desire that it be done? Yea, how could God have pleasure in one who either would not want to hear the will of God from the mercy seat, or having heard it and known it would hold to it only verbally? And would nevertheless boast that the mercy seat was there for his sake, or would present his own words and say that he had heard them from the mercy seat, yea, would curse and persecute everyone who would not believe the same; would not such boasting lead to his condemnation?

Or should we think, when Paul (1 Cor. 1) names Christ the justice and the wisdom of the believers or of Christians, that he means the outward Christ without the inward one, and not much more the inner together with the outer? Namely, since He is the Word of the Father, He manifests to us the true obedience, in which alone the Father has pleasure. He is the true bread of heaven which comes down from above, to nourish the souls of men. He says, "He who does not renounce all that he possesses cannot be his disciple." Item, says, "He who would follow me, let him deny himself." Item, "No one comes to the Father; but by me." Item, "I am the door to the sheepfold." Item, "I am the way, the truth, the life," and He testifies to all this in deed.[14]

To say nothing of the fact that Paul at this point is not speaking of Pharisees or scribes (as being the righteousness of Christ) but of himself and those like him who accept Him (Christ) in truth and hold to Him according to the instructions and demands of faith. But then what have we to do with those who so mightily boast of Christ with their mouth, claiming that Paul was writing about them, when they are the greatest persecutors of Christ and of Paul?

That the emperor ascribes himself so many kingdoms, what does that concern me, since I am a poor beggar? But when John the Baptist says (Jn. 1) that Christ is the Lamb, who takes upon Himself the sins of the world, he means, *insofar as* the world submits itself to Him in faith. Therefore he also says (Jn. 3), "He who believes the Son has eternal life, he who believes not the Son, will not see life." Similarly as well, when John says (1 Jn. 2), "He is our reconciliation," he means, namely for those who recognize Him. For although He is truly a reconciliation for the whole world, nevertheless this does not benefit anyone, except only those who recognize and accept Him, through faith. Those, however, who do this, keep the command of Christ. He who does not do this and still boasts of Christ as his reconciliation, he is a liar, for he has not yet ever known Christ, as John testifies. And should we think that Peter, when he says (1 Pet. 2), "He who himself offered our sin in his body upon the tree, that we should be without sin," meant that Christ thus sacrified for the sins of men so that men should be pronounced blameless by Him, whether they believe in Him or not, whether they forsake sinning or not, whether their will is changed by Him or not, as the work-righteous and the scribes think? God forbid. Why then should he say elsewhere (1 Pet. 1), "Whom you have not seen, and yet love; in whom you also believe and still do not behold"? Item, "And since you call on him as Father who judges, without respect of person, according to the works of each one, so conduct your walk with fear during the time of your pilgrimage." Item, "Blessed be God the Father of our Lord Jesus Christ, who according to his great mercy has regenerated us to a living hope, through the resurrection of Jesus Christ from the dead." They then who are without faith, without ceasing to sin, even more crassly than before,[15] yea, who just as before are of a servile and hateful disposition toward God and the neighbor, how could these apply this word of Peter to themselves, when Peter was writing not to them but to Christians?

In the same way one must understand the two words of Isaiah, for in Is. 28 he is also speaking of Christ in the power [of God]: "Behold, I lay a chosen precious cornerstone in Zion, and he who believes in him shall not come to shame." And Is. 8: "May the ruling Lord be your fear and your dread, and he will be your sanctification. But he shall be a stone of stumbling and a rock of offense to the two houses of Israel. . . ."

How then has Christ worked satisfaction for our sins? Answer: Not alone for our own, but for the sins of the whole world, insofar as the world believes in Him, and follows after Him according to the requirement of faith, as has been said. Yea, He as the head of His church, has done enough; yet He will nevertheless day by day again do enough[16] in His members and for them, until the end of the world, just as He had done from the beginnings [of the world] until His appearance. Therefore, when one speaks of justification through Christ, one must also speak of that faith, which cannot be without works of repentance, yea, not without love, which is an anointing. For such an anointed faith, which is given to one from the resurrection of the dead, is the only Christian faith, and is reckoned unto righteousness (Rom. 4).

Again when one speaks of works, one must preach not, after the manner of the work-righteous, the works of law but the works of faith; that is a turning away from works, creatures, and your own self, through faith in Christ the crucified one, not as what man can do from himself, but what he really can do in the power of faith; which thereby are not man's works but God's, since the willing and the ability to turn to God are not of man but the gift of God through Jesus Christ our Lord.

Verily, blessed be he who remains on the middle path, who turns aside neither to the work-righteous (who promised blessedness or the forgiveness of sins, through works done without faith, i.e., through that which, in one's works one thinks is one's own; thus they turn aside to the left and lead others that way,) preaching works in such a way that they think no more of faith, and wish neither to see nor to hear anything about faith, that it is necessary for salvation, so that all their works are like wild plums, i.e., ceremonies without faith. Nor to the side of the scribes, who although they have forsaken works, then turn aside to the right, and teach in the name of "gospel" a faith without works, and take the poor obedient Christ (who had no place to lay His head — Lk. 9. — who speaks without complaint or self-defense, Lk. 22, "nevertheless, Father, not my will but thy will be done") as their satisfaction, but will not hear what He says, Lk. 9: "Come, follow me." Item, Lk. 14: "He who does not forsake all that he possesses, cannot be my disciple." Item, Mk. 8: "He who would follow me, let him deny himself and take up his cross and follow me." Yes, the Father must also be a fanatic[17] to them, when He says, "That is my beloved Son, in whom I take satisfaction;[18] hear Him."

They make of Christ, after His humanity, what the pope has made out of the saints, namely a golden calf. Following the precedent of the Jews, that is, they confess Christ as son of David and then deny Him, yea, call Him a fanatic, since God's Word and Son was sent into the world, to manifest the obedience or righteousness of His Father not alone in words but also in works, so that all who would believe in Him should not perish in their death, but be delivered from death. All of their preaching and fruits are like prickly thistles. They say much about faith and yet know neither what Christ nor faith is. They reject works without faith in order to raise up faith without works. They would like to obey God with the soul and not also with the body, so that they might be without persecution. They believe that faith is a lazy and empty fiction, whereby they are also able to say that infants have faith, even though no works of faith can be discerned in them, even when they grow up. It would thus seem that the works of faith and the Holy Spirit were to curse when they hardly know how to speak, etc.[19] Oh, the miserable blindness! Although they write all of this not because they do not know better, but in order that they provide for their belly and maintain their honor. Thus one sees here so clearly how the beast, with seven heads and the ten horns, recuperates from its mortal wound; according to which the Roman school or curia, from which the Bread-Lord-God[20] and infant baptism originally come, are again defended as truths by the scribes.[21] To say nothing of many other things wherein the scribes again flatter the papists and set them up again as Christians. But that is how the second beast with the two horns, namely the band of the scribes, had to do, so that the earth and the men who live on it would again worship the first beast;[22] they had to reestablish the popish oil idols, that is the clergy; they had to throw down fire from heaven to banish and curse everyone who does not adhere to them, just as John had predicted it all. And this is precisely what he also saw, Rev. 17, how the ten horns on the beast would hate the harlot, and would leave her desolate and naked, would devour her flesh and burn her with fire, after God had put it in their hearts. The kingdom was to be given to the beast until the Word of God was all accomplished. Yea, that said ten horns, which [are] like kings, would take over the kingdom one hour after the beast, would come to an agreement to give power to the beast, would wage war with the Lamb and the Lamb would overcome them.[23] That is how in the last days from all the high schools, awakened by the Spirit, the scribes were to arise and to attack with great zeal the Roman Church, the congregation of the work-saints, seize everything, and consume all the gold, silver, and other goods which she had brought together, condemn her as heretical, but soon after they would again take the side of the beast, that is the Roman school, and defend it, and again cast away the kingdom of God which previously had come to them. Yea, these would then defend the beast against the Word of God and those who adhere to it, and would violently strive against the Lamb (i.e., Christ). Nevertheless the Lamb, Lord of all lords, Kings of all kings, would overcome them, together with His called and believing ones. And is that not, together with the papists, the abomination of desolation of which Dan. 9, Paul in 2 Thess. 2; Peter in 2 Pet. 2, and Christ in Mt. 24; Mk. 13; Lk. 17, clearly spoke, which now sits in the place of the saints, lets itself be worshiped as either gospel or Christendom since the work-saints say, "Behold, here is Christ!" The scribes call, "Behold, here is Christ!" And therefore blessed is he who goes out from said Babylon, that is, who believes neither the work-saints nor the scribes, but subjects himself with fear to the discipline of Christ, because the heavenly voice (Rev. 18; Is. 52; 2 Cor. 6) calls out and says, "Go out from her, my people, that you be not partakers of her sins, that you might not share in her torments, for her sin has echoed up to heaven."

Notes

1. First translated by John C. Wenger, *MQR*, XX, No. 4, October 1946, pp. 247 ff. Reprinted by Ferm, *op. cit.*, pp. 373 ff. The word used in the title, *Gnugthuung*, "doing enough," is the literal equivalent of the Latin *satisfactio*, the technical term for what is now most often called "atonement."

2. Rom. 3:23 ff. The "thesis" form of this first paragraph is reminiscent of the debating style of medieval universities and textbooks. Each quotation is introduced by "That . . ." and all but the first with the repetition sign *item* ("further"). In modern usage, "That Paul says, 'they are all together sinners . . .'" would be a dependent

clause after which one would expect: "means that. . . ." Here the entire first paragraph with its seven item statements stands toward the entire tract in such a way as such a subordinate clause stands toward the main affirmation. It is one side of the hypothesis for debate.

3. 1 Cor. 1:30. The style of Scripture text citation is erratic throughout the tract; the translation attempts to reproduce the variation. Some quotations are identified by the author, others are not.

4. The use of "scribes" to designate the theologians of the magisterial Reformation implies a period of living with the debate, so that there can be established polemical usages. The scribe is one learned in the Scriptures, who uses his erudition to avoid the meaning of the text he so learnedly interprets. "I say" is the sign of the transition from thesis to antithesis. (It also indicates single authorship; the first person appears once more later in the text.) First were listed the texts appealed to by the "scribes," and now come the other texts, likewise listed with *item*, on the author's side of the question. Beginning thus bluntly with a debating stance assumes that the reader is well aware of the polemic situation, a sign of authorship likely later than 1527. Cf. the terms used below, "On Hearing False Prophets or Anti-Christs," pp. 127ff.

5. *Bessert euch* renders "repent" with an emphasis on amendment of life.

6. "Further" here is not *item* but *weiter;* it marks the shift to a new mode of argument. Instead of simply aligning proof texts without comment, now a deduction or implication is drawn from each text.

7. The adjective *vermeinet* translated "seeming" means not "apparent" or "evident" but "falsely-thought-to-be." It points to the root meaning of the term *own*ership / *property* / *Eigentum,* "that which is one's own." That which we call our own, the author says, only seems, by deception, to be ours; in reality it is God's and therefore not ours to renounce or to keep. "Creatures" means all created values, especially material goods. Faith thus renounces the deluded effort to affirm one's autonomy and ownership.

8. "The Christian faith" here means specifically the Apostles' Creed, which most Anabaptists continued to use. "Fellowship of the saints" is the same as "community."

9. The shifting between "us" and "you" is in the original. At one point the writer paraphrases, including himself and the reader as "us" to whom the epistle is addressed; then he falls back into direct quotation.

10. Literally "if Christ has *done enough* in such a way . . . that nothing more is lacking. . . ." This use of the term "enough" illuminates the issue under debate. One major theme of the conversation between Anabaptists and the magisterial Reformers was the strong ethical concern of the Anabaptists. Cf. above pp. 87 ff. Here it is visible that the Reformers are understood as arguing that to make such ethical demands is to jeopardize the uniqueness and adequacy of the work of Christ. Christ's sacrifice *did enough;* to claim that we must do something more denies this. Thus *satisfactio* is not just the label for the doctrine; the doctrine is exposited by exegeting the word. The author's answer is not based on a word but on the many scriptural imperatives to do something.

11. Phil. 2:17: "If I am to be poured out as a libation upon the offering of your faith."

12. Paragraph divisions are our own; there are none in the *SB* text. Here a new type of argument begins. The suffering of the believers extends the suffering of Christ, in express application of the Pauline concept of the body of Christ. This thought is widespread in early Anabaptism, cf. Conrad Grebel's letter to Thomas Müntzer (Williams and Mergal, *SAW,* p. 84): "Christ must suffer still more in His members." Cf. also Ethelbert Stauffer, "The Anabaptist Theology of Martyrdom." *MQR* XIX, 1945, pp, 179 ff. Here we observe that this linkage of suffering with the concept of the body extends as well into the Lord's Supper.

13. The acceptance of suffering is not merely a test of loyalty but also an eschatological event. The prophets and apostles and Christ all predicted the suffering of the friends of God. "Friend of God" is one of the favorite Anabaptist designations of godliness.

14. Some of these texts were cited before; then it was to prove Jesus' demand for obedience; now it is His claim to unique authority.

15. As Wenger says, the reference here is to the fact that in some quarters the popular impact of Protestant teaching against the prevalent legalism was to foster a relaxation of moral discipline, sometimes in the name of "grace alone," cf. above Schleitheim pp. 35 f. The writer argues that that libertinism is allied to the way the "scribes" argue against his ethical concern.

16. Although the phrase *gnug gethan* is plain lay language, the reader will still hear in it the theological overtones of *satisfactio / atonement*. Thus it is all the more striking when the writer restates the meaning of Christian ethics as part of this context: Christian behavior, especially suffering, is Christ continuing to *do enough* in His members.

17. "Fanatic" renders *Schwürmer*, an equivalent of *Schwärmer*. Here and again in the next paragraph, all that it means is the claim that God demands of man an obedience which partakes of the character of the humanity of Jesus. The original meaning of *Schwärmer* emphasized disorderly enthusiasm, confused and erratic claims of illumination; this note is absent in our context. The writer neither accepts nor rejects the term; he simply says that his critics, if they apply it to him, would have to apply it to God and Jesus too.

18. *Gnügen*.

19. Wenger calls attention to *Ausbund* hymn 46, stanza 2: "Now children in the street swear by the blood of Christ."

20. The Bread-Lord-God is the transubstantiated host, here referred to as epitome of superstitious apostasy.

21. The claim that the magisterial Reformers had begun teaching the truth (to which the Anabaptists continued to hold) and had then fallen back into traditional positions is a standard Anabaptist interpretation of early Reformation history. Here it is seen as fulfillment of the predictions of Revelation.

22. Rev. 13:11 f.

23. The citations from Rev. 17 are first vv. 16-18, then 12-14. What for John the seer lay in the distant future is now the recent past. The author sees himself, and the whole drama of the Reformation, as the fulfillment of the apocalyptic plan.

VIII

On Two Kinds of Obedience

The Text

There are two kinds of obedience; servile and filial.[1] The filial springs forth from the love of the Father even if no other reward should follow; yea, even if the Father should wish to damn the child. The servile springs out of love of reward or of self. The filial ever does as much as it can, apart from any command. The servile does as little as it can; yea, does nothing unless it be commanded. The filial can never do enough for Him; the servile thinks it is always doing too much.[2] The filial rejoices in the Father's chastisement even if it has transgressed in nothing. The servile wants never to be chastised by the Lord even though it does nothing right. The filial has its treasure and its righteousness in the Father whom it obeys solely in order to manifest His righteousness.[3] The treasure and the righteousness of the servile are the works that it does to acquire righteousness. The filial remains in the house and inherits all that the Father has; the servile is driven out and receives its justly prescribed reward.[4] The servile looks to the outward and prescribed command of his Lord; the filial is attentive to the inner witness and the Spirit. The servile is imperfect and therefore his Lord has no pleasure in him; the filial strives thereafter and becomes perfect, and therefore the Father cannot reject him.

The filial is not contrary to the servile, as it might appear, but better and higher.[5] Therefore let him who is in the servile, seek after a better [obedience] which is the filial, which needs the servile not at all.

The servile is Moses and brings forth Pharisees and scribes.[6] The filial is Christ and makes children of God. The servile busies himself either with the ceremonies which Moses commanded or with those which men themselves have invented.[7] The filial is busy with the love of God and the neighbor; yet he will also sometimes subject himself to the ceremonies for the sake of the serfs[8] in order better to instruct them and bring them to sonship. The servile makes self-willed and vengeful people; the filial makes tolerant and mild. The servile is heavy-spirited, would wish to come soon to the end of the work; the filial is light, takes no account of duration. The servile is malevolent; wishes good to no one but himself. The filial wishes that all men could be as he.[9] The servile is the old covenant, and has the promise of temporal blessedness, i.e., the creature. The filial is the new covenant which has the promise of eternal blessedness, of the Creator Himself. The servile is a beginning and a preparation for blessedness; the filial is the end and completeness itself. The servile endured for a time; the filial shall stand eternally. The servile was a figure and a shadow; the filial is body and truth.

The servile was instituted to reveal and to increase sin;[10] the filial follows to do away with and blot out the revealed and increased sin. For if man is ever to escape from sin, he must hate it. If he is to hate it he must first know it.[11] If he is to know it, there must be something which stirs up the hidden sin and makes it known.[12] Such is the Law, or Scripture, for as much as the Law demands, so much more man turns away from God to that which he has done, and justifies himself thereby, as an achievement of his own, clings to it as to his treasure. The greater such love is, the more and greater his hate grows toward God and the neighbor. For the more man clings to the creature, the farther he is from God. The more he desires the creatures, the less he desires the Creator. But the Law gives a man occasion to separate himself all the more from God, and not on its own account (for the Law is good) but because of the sin which is in man.

Which is also the reason Paul says that the Law was given that it might increase sin, so that sin would thereby be known; yea, the Law is the strength of sin,[13] and therefore just as servile obedience (i.e., obedience of the Law) leads man to the greatest hatred toward God and of neighbor, so also the filial [obedience] is a certain way whereby to escape such hatred and to receive the love of God and neighbor. Therefore, the one administers death, the other administers life. The former is the Old Testament, the latter the New.

In the Old only he was liable to judgment who killed; but in the New he who is wrathful with his brother.[14] The Old permitted one to divorce his wife for whatever reason; the New not at all, except for adultery. The Old permits swearing, as long as one swears rightly; the New will know nothing of swearing. The Old had a specified vengeance; the New does not resist evil. The Old permitted hatred for the enemy; the New loves him who hates it, blesses him who curses it, prays for those who wish it ill, gives its alms in such a manner that the left hand does not know what the right has done, speaks its prayer secretly without evident and excessive babbling of the mouth, judges and condemns no one, draws the splinter from the eye of his brother after first casting the beam out of its own; fasts without pomp and show; is like a light that stands on a candlestick and illuminates everyone in the house; is like a city that is built upon a hill, visible from all sides; is like good salt that does not become tasteless, serves not man but God alone, is just like a good eye which illuminates the whole body, is not anxious for clothing nor for food, but does its daily honest work; does not cast pearls before swine nor what is holy before dogs; seeks, asks, and knocks, and thus finds and receives and has the door opened to it; enters through the narrow way and the strait gate, protects himself from Pharisees and scribes as from false prophets; is a good tree and brings forth good fruit; does the will of his Father, hearing what he should do, and then doing it.

It[15] is built on Christ the chief corner stone and stands

against all the gates of hell; that is, against the wrathful judgment of the Pharisees, the mighty ones of this world and the scribes. It is a house and a temple of God, against which no wind and no water can do anything. It stands fast, even though all else argues against it, that it is not what it claims to be, it must finally be acknowledged by the same[16] to be a dwelling of God, though it is now maligned by the Pharisees and scribes as a habitation of the devil; yea, it will finally hear, "Behold the tabernacle of God among men, he will dwell with them, they shall be his people, and God himself will be with them as their God" etc.[17] So it will be said of the house of the Pharisees and scribes, "She is fallen, she is fallen, Babylon the great, and become a dwelling place of devils and a vessel of all unclean spirits and of all unclean and hateful birds, etc."[18] But to God (by whom everything which boasts it is not, will be shown for what it is) be all honor, praise and glory, through His beloved Son, our Lord and Brother Jesus Christ, Amen.

Notes

1. First translated by J. C. Wenger in *MQR*, XXI, Jan. 1947, p. 18, and frequently reprinted, including Fosdick, *op. cit.*, p. 296.

2. Since *Gehorsam* ("obedience") is masculine, these sentences read constantly, "He does. . . , he rejoices. . . , etc." This pushes the writer in the direction of personification. "Obedience" becomes nearly identical with "a person obeying." At this particular point the Wenger translation spells out the personification in a paraphrase: ". . . he who renders servile obedience thinks he is constantly doing too much for Him." Also at later points, the Wenger translation wavers between the personified "he" and the abstract "it" (obedience). The present translation uses "it" consistently except in the third paragraph where "he" is used; the reader should keep in mind that the two aspects of meaning are both present throughout.

3. I.e., with no consideration of merit.

4. Wenger interprets this passage through the seeming allusion to the parable of the Prodigal Son and thus translates "the servile wishes to reject this and receive his lawful reward." But the allusion is only seeming: the servile obedience is said here to be driven out (*vertrieben*), which does not fit the parable.

5. This sentence is the key to the tension which the tract attempts to define. The difference lies not between right and wrong, truth and heresy, but between two levels of maturity or of authenticity. (Paragraph divisions are the translator's, usually following Wenger: there are none in the original.)

6. Although borrowed from the biblical vocabulary, the reference to "Pharisees and scribes" is to contemporary religious leaders, with special reference to their professional and social status. The same usage is evident in other tracts in this collection.

7. "Ceremonies" is the technical term in the Zwinglian Reformation and among its Anabaptist descendants for visible ritual usages; prescribed prayers, use of salt, oil, holy water, vestments, "images," processions, etc. . . , but also for the Mosaic ordinances.

8. Here the device of personification is abandoned for the sake of direct allusion to spiritually immature persons. The "ceremonies" or worship rituals are theologically and morally neutral. It would be better to do away with these in order to overcome superstition: but since they are morally neutral, it is possible to make concessions to avoid offending the immature. This reference indicates that even the most radical Anabaptist was not closed in principle to such a "pedagogical" accommodation to the common man's limited understanding, for a limited time. The "serfs" are obviously those still living on the servile level of obedience.

9. Here the personification of obedience as "he" is the most complete, by virtue of the parallel with "men."

10. Rom. 5:20.

11. I.e., recognize it as such.

12. Cf. Rom. 7:7 ff. Here we perceive again that servile obedience is not totally to be rejected. It leads to filial obedience as Law leads to gospel. With this in mind, it might be good to translate the title as does R. Friedmann, "*Twofold* Obedience," (*loc. cit.*, p. 89).

13. 1 Cor. 15:56.

14. This paragraph is clearly modeled after Mt. 5. At this point the pairing servile / filial is juxtaposed upon another, that of the Old Testament and the New. "Testament" here means primarily a "covenant" or "dispensation," a new phase or level in God's working with men, instituted by Christ. Only in a derived way does this correspond to the distinction between the Old Testament and New Testament as texts or as Scripture.

15. Here Wenger supplies as subject of the sentence, "the church of true believers." This makes a meaningful sentence, but there is no clear reason why a subject must be supplied. The subject "it" could very well refer to "The New" of the previous paragraph, or the "filial obedience" of the first half of the tract.

16. I.e., but "all else that argues against it." Here there may be an allusion to 1 Pet. 2:12.

17. Rev. 21:3.

18. 18:2.

IX

On False Prophets and Evil Overseers

Introduction

Especially for these last items included in *SB* is the likelihood of Sattler's authorship uncertain. The only ground for assuming his authorship is their inclusion in the *SB*. There is no definitive internal evidence for or against Sattler, but analysis of the polemic elements of these two tracts tends to point away from an origin before May 1527.

a) Frequent reference to "papists and Lutherans" in the texts indicates that the Anabaptist movement has spread from the Reformed regions (Switzerland, Strasbourg, Marburg) into the areas where the predominant state churches were those named. Sattler would not have called "Lutheran" the Reformers with whom he dealt. The language of the *Seven Articles* is "popish" and "repopish (or antipopish)."

b) Nor would Sattler likely have been in a context where the balanced weighing of the Catholic and Lutheran errors against each other would be called for or possible.[1]

c) There are differences in literary form between these tracts and the more clearly authentic Sattler writings, such as the way Scripture allusions are cited. This would in itself not be a conclusive argument, since every reprinting changed such details somewhat.

d) The error of the "false prophets" and "evil overseers" is that they advocate conformity to the larger hostile society. This advocacy is based either on the claim that they have some kind of special revelation or on their interpretation of certain Bible passages.[2] In the time of Sattler, the danger of false prophetism was equally great on the opposite side, namely that of libertinism, as is indicated especially in the introduction of the *Brotherly Union*. Although the two dangers are closely linked in Sattler's thought and in the way Schleitheim responded to them, only the former has left a trace in these polemic documents. This would indicate that when this tract was written, the time of the struggle with enthusiasm on the left fringes of southern Anabaptism was past.

The Texts
A. *On hearing False Prophets or Anti-Christs*[3]

What love both toward God and toward man forbids and makes obligatory (— since love wills but one thing, and is opposed to all which is contrary thereto),[4] he who is a true Christian will not wish to dissolve or to have free. But now love commands, Mt. 7:15, 16, that one should protect himself from false prophets who come to us in sheep's clothing (i.e., hung about with letters[5]); she [i.e., love] would certainly not want to free us to run after them and to be subject[6] to them in counterfeit hypocrisy.[7]

And yet how God must complain, through nearly all the prophets, with great zeal, that His people do not want to hear, but rather run after the false prophets, who can offer nothing but dreams and the opinions of their own hearts. Jer. 23:27; Ezek. 13. But do we want to believe that the sheep of Christ can recognize the voice of the mercenary? Jn. 10. Should then the living Christ be found amidst the dead Pharisees and scribes, the desolation and abomination? Lk. 24. Should not a people seek their own God? Is. 8. But shall we ask the dead for the living? Mt. 26.[8] How can the sweet dough of Christ and the sour dough of the Pharisees and Sadducees agree? Mk. 16.[9] How does Christ harmonize with Belial? Or the temple of God and that of idols? 2 Cor. 6: The yoke of Christ and that of the anti-Christ? Mt. 13.[10]

Unless such idols might sometime speak the Word of God — though it does stand written, the idols of the Gentiles are silver and gold, the handiwork of men, they have eyes and see not, they have a mouth and do not speak, Ps. 115.

What profits the image that its maker has carved? Or the idol which teaches deceit, in which his maker so puts his trust, that he fabricates dumb idols? Woe to him who says to the wood, "Awake" and to the dumb stone, "Stand up!" Should it teach something? Behold it is laid over in silver and gold and has no breath in it. Hab. 2.

Unless both,[11] the papist and Lutheran, yea, also all others, who are of their nature, creatures who proclaim letter for spirit and the command of men for the command of God, when Christ speaks clearly to such people, "You brood of vipers, how can you speak good when you are evil; whereof the heart is full, thereof the mouth overflows," Mt. 12. Wherefore He also then says, "Beware of the scribes, who walk around in long garments, and receive greetings in the market place, and gladly take the highest seats in the synagogues, and eat up the houses of widows, etc." Mk. 12. Therefore Paul also says, "Beware of the dogs. Look out for the evil workers, watch out for the circumcision," etc. Phil. 3. But now it is said everywhere (in order not to be persecuted by the false prophets and to avoid the cross) that such a prohibition of love does not forbid the bodily attendance but only the assent and agreement of the heart,[12] as it stands written, "Test everything, and accept that which is good." 1 Thess. 2.

Answer: The man who wantonly and willingly takes poison into his mouth thinking that because of his expertness nothing could go wrong if he swallowed it, but misjudged the amount and died, everyone would obviously say that he died intentionally. Further: if any man would openly look at the fruit of an evil tree or would see that many men had died from eating a certain food, and then would desire first of all to try the tree or the food to see if it was good or bad, and would die: again, everyone would say that such a one merited his death. Or would it be appropriate that a shepherd, when for two days a wolf had run among his sheep and done great damage, should on the third day accept the wolf as keeper of the sheep, with the hope that this time he would behave? He who (when the evil has been sufficiently demonstrated) intentionally wants to test it again by running after it, let him look out that he not break his neck falling into the pit which was prepared and stubbornly entangle himself in the already laid snare.

Everywhere the apostles of the angel of darkness are now speaking, having disguised themselves as apostles of Christ, 2 Cor. 11, they say to all who sincerely wish to walk in the way, that they should, like the birds, fly to the mountain; then they draw their bow and lay their arrow on it, so that in the dark they may shoot to death the souls of the living. Ps. 11. Indeed it does stand written: "He will command the angels for thy sake that they take thee up with their hands, that thou mightest not strike thy foot against a stone," Ps. 91. Yet it also stands written, "Thou shalt not test God thy Lord." Deut. 6. If Dinah the daughter of Jacob had remained at home and not gone out walking to look at the daughters of the land, she would not have become a harlot. Gen. 34. But if someone has such a great desire to listen intentionally to proven false prophets, he has the worst evil of all dwelling within his own bosom, which will, as long as he does not listen to it, make him so unhappy with its unceasing prattle, that he will not know how to escape. One should not, as they say,[13] put the louse on the fur; it gets in anyway. It is therefore Christian and prudent in these most evil days to hold oneself to what Christ says: "If then anyone says to you, 'See, here is Christ, or there,' you shall not believe it. For false Christs and false prophets shall arise and do great signs and wonders, and will seduce into error if possible even the elect." Mt. 24. The abomination will now be manifested openly in the holy city. Dan. 9, 11. Even those who for a long time have let themselves be reproached as brothers[14] will also begin publicly to pour out their wrath against the miserable, broken little flock of the Lord, so that by their own fruit they might be recognized before the whole world, confessing in deed that they for a long time had hidden themselves under the trumped-up sheep's clothing of Scripture.[15] Mt. 7. Yea [it is Christian and prudent],[16] to do as the Lord commanded through Isaiah saying, "Go, O my people, into thy chamber, shut the door after thee, and remain hidden there a little while until the wrath passes over." Is. 26. For after a little time he who shall come will come and will not tarry. The righteous man, however, will live by his faith and should he deviate, my soul will have no pleasure in him. Heb. 10. Yea, he says, if the just man abandons righteousness and behaves wrongly, practicing all the abominations of the godless, shall that man live? Ezek. 18. But the God of peace and the Father of mercy will graciously deliver both us and you, by the revealing of His Son, our Lord Jesus Christ, from the contrary powers of darkness and the anti-Christ. Amen.

B. Evil Overseers[17]

Grace and peace from God our Father and our Lord Jesus Christ. Amidst so many tribulations (most beloved brothers and sisters in the Lord) which arise in our times, this also is happening to us, that so many overseers become hindseers[18] pretending that without a calling they have come into the service they render, and running without a commandment of the Lord.[19] Because tribulation daily increases against the truth and the Lord (as we see it) delays His coming, it is not enough for them to have been found unfaithful with the talent committed to them and the work they have accepted in the vineyard, just like their ancestors the scribes, but they also want to take away from the Lord everything that had been gained at interest by their talent, yea, to destroy all the work already done. In their merited death and weakness they wish not only to kill the weak but also to weaken the strong and confuse them with scandal, not regarding what Christ says, Mt. 18: "he who offends one of the least of these, or hampers those who believe on me, it would be better for him that a millstone were hung around his neck and he were sunk in the sea where it is the deepest." They say that one can without harm listen to the papist or Lutheran preachings, since they will have it,[20] in order to affront no one, even though Christ so earnestly commands, Mt. 24, that we should flee from such desolation and abomination and in no way turn back to it, with a faithful warning to remember Lot's wife, Lk. 21. And even though Paul speaks with such clear words, 2 Cor. 6, Do not pull under the same yoke with unbelievers, for what has righteousness in common with unrighteousness? To say nothing of how John, together with all the prophets, so earnestly commands us to go out of such a Babylon so that we might not be partakers of her plagues: Rev. 18; Is. 52; Jer. 51.

Since, however, they say as well, against themselves and against the truth, that infant baptism is indifferent[21] and one can baptize infants without detriment to the truth, it is certain that they are in league with the Lutherans, hoping perhaps henceforth to be able to live without the cross. Even if infant baptism were not directly counter to the baptism of Christ, and now Christ, Mt. 17, but also the anti-Christ or hireling, Jn. 10, were to be heard,[22] to say nothing of the commandments of men which are so manifoldly forbidden,[23] Mt. 15; Col. 2; Tit. 1; 2 Cor. 2; Gal. 5. But is that not, as Peter says, according to the word of the proverb, to devour again what the dog has vomited? 2 Pet. 2. May God uproot and cut off such, because with such a blasphemy they attack the house and the temple of God. How would the Lutherans want the more conveniently (to speak according to the flesh) to escape and to do more harm than when they say that what they did against the papacy was done with the word of faith? They did not do it according to the command and the calling of God but their own wantonness.[24] Therefore everything is wrong, which they did and taught in this manner, as also their fathers did, when they said, they did not know if the baptism of John was of God or of man, Mt. 21; yet they said the same against their own consciences.

We hope therefore that we have warned all brothers and sisters in the Lord, who have separated themselves from this desolation and abomination by accepting the truth, so that you might not let yourself be driven away from the hope which is set before you, by the false scheming and inconstancy of the overseers. Pray the Lord of the harvest that He might send forth faithful laborers into His work, yea, that the master of the house might go out at the eleventh hour and hire for his vineyard those who stood idle all day, so that all which is still undone in the vineyard might be completed.

May the Father of peace and all mercy graciously keep both us and you from all error through the intercession of His Child, our Lord Jesus Christ. Amen.

Notes

1. See above p. 116; below esp. pp. 128, 131. Cf. p. 113f, his understanding of Paul on the matter of justification.

2. Cf. below esp. p. 129.

3. Previous translation from *SB* by John C. Wenger, in *MQR*, XXI, Oct. 1947, p. 276.

4. Literally: ([since love but one thing] wills, and to all which is contrary to that one thing, is enemy). The German original has been rendered quite unintelligible by the omission of the section set above in brackets; it can be clearly reconstructed on the basis of the Dutch (*BRN*, V, p. 637). This indicates that the Dutch is based on a different original, presumably earlier, than the printing extant in *SB*.

5. The meaning of "hung about with letters" is unclear. Might it conceivably refer to academic degrees? A more likely meaning would be that false prophets claim to base their teachings on specific biblical texts. This probability, that the case made by the false prophets was couched in biblicistic terms, would strengthen our general impression that the Anabaptists did not consider themselves as vigorous literalists. It is a matter of fact quite striking that although these false teachers are referred to as "prophets" there is no indication that their claim to a hearing is based upon pretended visions or special revelations. This argues against the assumption, made among others by Cramer, that the specific adversaries here in view would be visionary persons of the type of David Joris.

6. "To be subject" here designates not politically forced subjugation but the listeners' voluntary acceptance of the false prophets' teaching.

7. "Counterfeit hypocrisy" is an emphatic redundancy, not a double negative.

8. The scriptural allusion intended here is unclear. J. C. Wenger suggests Lk. 24:5.

9. Perhaps Mt. 16:16 ff. is meant.

10. Wenger suggests Mt. 11:29 f.; but there is no yoke of anti-Christ mentioned there. These three incorrect citations are further evidence of the likely existence of an earlier printing. They would more easily have arisen as misprints in a reprinting from an earlier pamphlet than in a first edition.

11. This phrase marks the beginning of a conditional subordinate clause, which is left dangling or rather transformed en route into an affirmative sentence. The translation attempts to reproduce the non-grammatical construction.

12. Cf. above, *Schleitheim Confession* (IV), p. 52 n. 63. Now obviously some were advocating outward attendance at state church services on the ground that one could attend without agreeing.

13. This parenthetical "(as one says)" introduces an allusion to a current proverb. The use of nonscriptural quotations is not frequent in our materials.

14. I.e., some who formerly bore the reproach of Anabaptism ("brothers" was a technical term, used also by their adversaries to designate the Anabaptists) will now share in denouncing them. Thus the ranks of "false prophets" can include former Anabaptist leaders.

15. The "sheep's clothing of Scripture" does not refer simply to the wolf's disguise as alluded to in Mt. 7, but rather to a scriptural (i.e., Anabaptist) position which was itself artificial and proud. "Scripture" here cannot mean the biblical *words;* it must denote the biblical *position.* The "of" is appositive not possessive.

16. The original has here the simple infinitive: "Yea, to do as the Lord commanded. . . ." The Dutch translation (*BRN*, V, 640) supplies a subject: "they do . . ." which must refer to the false Christs and false prophets. As editor Cramer notes, this makes no sense. Wenger supplies the subject in the second person: "Yea, do thou . . ." which makes more sense but is grammatically unwarranted; the tract is not addressed to a "thou." It thus seems most fitting to assume that the writer still has in mind the prefatory clause "it is Christian and prudent" which introduced the preceding point.

17. The text of *SB*, which we follow in this translation, has only a small break in the text at this point. The closing and opening greetings to the reader, however, indicate that this is the beginning of an originally separate tract. This is confirmed by the Dutch translation, which thereby again (cf. above note 4) indicates that there was an earlier, less corrupted German printing of the *SB* material.

The difference between the "prophets" and the "overseers" would seem to be in the nature of their claim to a hearing within the Anabaptist movement. The evil overseers are Anabaptist leaders tending to relativize the Anabaptist identity; the false prophets are the spokesmen of Lutheran and Catholic alternatives. The tone and the themes of the texts are so familiar that we do no violence to them when we follow our extant text (and the early Hutterite manuscript copies) in running them together. "On Evil Overseers" was also first translated by J. C. Wenger, *loc. cit.,* p. 280.

18. The term here rendered "overseer" is *Vorsteher,* literally "forestander," one who *stands before* the church, or presides. The play on words in the text changes this to "behind-stander"; instead of *pre*siding, these false leaders *post*side.

19. Jer. 23:21. "Calling" here means congregational authorization of the kind referred to in Schleitheim Art. V. To "pretend to have come without a calling" is then to claim ministerial status without ever having been called by a congregation. This concern for due credentials in the ministry contradicts the claim of the magisterial churchmen that Anabaptism was unconcerned for order.

20. The second "they" in the sentence means vaguely "the [papist and Lutheran] authorities" who press the Anabaptists to attend church, and is not identical with the first "they" in the sentence. A more literal translation would be "one will have it so."

21. *Mittelmessig.* By the time of this text Lutheran theology had developed a clear doctrine of *adiaphora,* labeling those issues to which Scripture does not speak, and which may be freely dealt with as seems best on the basis of common sense and the common good.

22. I.e., if the biblical text or teaching regarding the hireling were to be heard and obeyed.

23. I.e., if we were to respect the clear prohibition of respecting the commandments of men.

24. The claim that many of those who favored the Reformation did so not out of respect for the Word of God but in order to be freed from the constraints of Catholic piety and moral discipline was a criticism not limited to the Anabaptists. Zwingli said as much already in late 1524 in his "Who gives occasion for Turmoil," cf. above p. 46, note 9.

X

Epistle from Melchior Rinck[1]

The Text

Grace and peace from God our Father and [from our] Lord Jesus Christ! Beloved in the Lord, be it known to you that I, Melchior Rinck, and Anthonius Jacob, brothers in the Lord, imprisoned at Hayne[2] for the sake of the truth, are still lively [frisch] and well by the power of the Almighty God, and hope to stand [true] to the end to both doctrines, the baptism and the supper of Christ,[3] and to all else that belongs with them, although the papist and Luther's party seeks[4] for such a long time to drive us away from the same. May God redeem His own out of the power of both. Amen.

Note[5]
Let the Children Come to Me, etc., Mk. 10

Just as one cannot damn children on account of unbelief, likewise one cannot declare them saved on the grounds of faith, since one cannot preach and they cannot hear. Just as they neither know nor hate evil, so are they without knowledge and love of the good.

He who so loves the children of nature that he hates and calls "fanatics" the children of the spirit . . .[6]

Or he who brings natural children to Christ in such a way that he will not let the children of the new birth come to Christ, he does not love children who are children by nature but hates them; for he brings them not to Christ but to Belial. He wants to retain through infant baptism what he never had, namely the blessing, and wants to escape what is already around his neck, namely the curse, because he loves the creature and himself in such a way that he rejects the Creator. Verily, that both the work-saints and the scribes[7] strive so mightily concerning infant baptism, is not done out of love for the children, for they are precisely the ones who consume the bread that belongs to the children and to the poor orphans, and fatten themselves on it; they are doing it rather in order to retain their craftiness, honor and power, false Christianity, which they have all acquired by setting up such baptism. For Satan senses well that as soon as a congregation is established, in which not only with mouth and heart but also with deeds and love the obedience of Christ is demonstrated, then his darkness can no longer stand in the face of such light, as it is manifest, that his gospel and Christendom is the abomination of desolation.[8] Would not a city soon be destroyed and a sheepfold soon laid waste, if one would introduce the enemy of the city in his young years, raise him up in the city, so that he would know all its customs, until he comes to his maturity, and thus would be able to attack the city not from the outside in (where it would not be possible to win over against her) but from the inside out (what no city can withstand)? Would it then be possible after the deed, to get such an enemy out of the city, after he had bound to himself a major portion of the citizens, or someone from outside, to whom the city out of fear had become vassal? Or would it be possible to keep such a one within without surrendering the city?

Likewise if a shepherd were to take a young wolf or lion or bear into the sheepfold, and raise it with the sheep, would they not finally, once they were grown, destroy both the shepherd and the sheep? Yea, they would themselves want to be both shepherd and sheep. Now the scribes are going about driving out of their congregations those whom they know are wolves, bears, and lions, so they will well experience what infant baptism has brought about.[9] But the dogs will not do it, for they too have now become dumb, and they themselves would rather attack the sheep with greater fury than before, but what they cannot destroy they with great concern beg the lions for help, preferring to remain vassals if they cannot conquer.

Notes

1. Melchior Rinck, pastor in Thuringia and Hesse, was under the influence of Martin Luther and then of Thomas Müntzer, before he came in contact with Anabaptism, perhaps in early 1527 when Hans Denck and others were in Worms. Our sketchy knowledge of his life (*ME*, IV, 336) does not account for the period between Müntzer's fall and 1527. He was sometimes called "the Greek"; presumably an indication of humanistic training. For the sake of a complete rendering of the materials of *SB* we include these last two brief items, both clearly later than Sattler. This letter is so brief that one must ask why it was included in a collection of tracts of this kind. Was the collection perhaps reprinted especially for the parts of the German Anabaptist movement where Rinck's leadership was central?

2. Rinck's several imprisonments are recorded in Günther *Wiedertäuferakten, 1527-1626*. Marburg, 1951, pp. 3 ff., 31 ff., 41 ff., 261, 270. The editor suggests ca. 1530 as the date for the one document which refers to Haina, near Frankenberg on the Eder, as the place of imprisonment (*ibid.*, 31).

3. It is remarkable that for the Anabaptists the Lord's Supper is often mentioned as of equal significance with baptism, even though the persecution to which they were subjected focused almost uniquely on the latter.

4. The verb here is singular. The argument would seem to be that Catholic and Lutheran powers alike were seeking to bring Anabaptists away from their faith, not that both confessions were actually dealing with him in Haina. This reference to both groups, as united in their hostility to Anabaptists though quite different between themselves, is already noted in the preceding documents. (Above p. 117 f.)

5. Scholarly comment on this text has assumed that the following treatise ("*Nota*") is a part of the epistle from Rinck. The text as preserved in *SB* and *BRN*, V, gives no support for this assumption. The epistle is separated from the following text more than the two treatises on false prophets and evil overseers are separated. Content and collocation may provide circumstantial arguments for assuming that Rinck wrote the *Nota*, or even that the two once circulated together before being brought into *SB*; but the format of *SB* does not itself prove this.

6. This incomplete sentence is followed by "item," which in another context (see above pp. 108 ff.) marks the beginning of a long list of parallel points; here, however, the second beginning goes on to conclude the statement.

7. This usage parallels that of the earlier tracts: cf. p. 119, note 4, p. 120, note 21. This pairing of Lutherans and Catholics is all that links this "note" to the Rinck epistle; and the pairing "scribes [Reformers] and work-saints [Catholics]" links it as well to the other tracts in the collection (see above pp. 116 ff.). This might indicate that if Sattler is not the author of these other tracts, Rinck might be.

8. It is most significant that in the entire volume of the *SB*, as well as the earlier tracts which made it up, constituting a major segment of the printed spiritual nourishment available to the early south German Anabaptists, there is no extended discussion of baptism as a theological or liturgical issue in its own right. Even this text, which begins as if it were to be that, moves on immediately to see the baptism issue as related to the apostasy of the church and to conflicting views of Reformation.

9. The "scribes" are the Reformers, trying against impossible odds to rid the church of unbiblical abuses (the beasts of prey); the "dogs" are the clergy. According to the writer, the Reformers should perceive the wrongness of infant baptism, since it was thereby that the bearers of all the abuses were given entry into the churches.

XI

When Christ with His Teaching True

Introduction

The South-German Anabaptist *Ausbund,* still in use today by the Old Order Amish in North America, can be called the "oldest hymnbook in continuous usage in any Christian church" (*ME,* I, 191). The nucleus of this collection was gathered by a handful of Anabaptists in prison in Passau 1535-40. By 1583 the collection was printed with the same name and nearly the same contents as today. One didactic hymn on the theme of discipleship is specifically attributed to Sattler in the *Ausbund* itself; another is attributed to him by later tradition.[1]

The translation offered here is as literal as possible, making no poetic pretensions. In many Anabaptist "hymns," including these two, there is no claim to aesthetic merit; the rhythm and rhyme are simply helpful mnemonic and didactic tools.

It is thus not in disrespect for the original intent and function of these hymns when in this context we center attention upon their discursive substance, leaving to the poets the task of a genuinely poetic reconception. Myron Augsburger has worked partial poetic versions into his novel, *Pilgrim Aflame.*[2]

The reader can support a sense of rhyme and rhythm by reference to the German text printed in parallel. Here the (formally modernized) text of today's *Ausbund* has been used, rather than seeking to restore an original sixteenth-century spelling which would be more difficult for the modern reader.

The Amish have preserved and transmitted the *Ausbund* tunes unwritten for these four centuries; as is normal with such aural/oral transmission, this has led to gradual changes and to geographical variations, generally in the direction of slowing the melodic line and almost hiding it under various kinds of embellishment.[3] The original tunes used with Anabaptist hymns were well-known tunes, both new and old, both "sacred" and "secular."[4] It happens that both the tunes used in the hymns attributed to Sattler were known as hymn tunes.

When Christ with His Teaching True

Als Christus mit Sein'r Wahren Lehr

1. Als Christus mit sein'r wahren Lehr
   Versammlet hatt' ein kleines Heer,
   Sagt er dass jeder mit Geduld
   Ihm täglich's Kreutz nachtragen sollt.

2. Und sprach: Ihr liebe Jünger mein,
   Ihr solet allzeit munter seyn,
   Auf Erden auch nichts lieben mehr,
   Denn mich und folgen meiner Lehr.

3. Die Welt die wird euch stellen nach,
   Und anthun manchen Spott und Schmach,
   Verjagen und auch sagen frey,
   Wie dass der Satan in euch sey.

Tune: *Christe qui lux est et dies:* Version Klug[5]

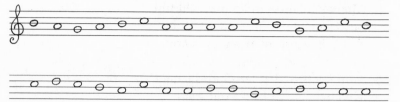

Christe qui lux est et dies: Version Sarum[6]

When Christ with His Teaching True: [7] verbatim rendering

1. When Christ with His teaching true
   Had gathered a little flock[8]
   He said that each with patience
   Must daily follow Him bearing his cross.

2. And said: You, my beloved disciples,
   Must be ever courageous
   Must love nothing on earth more than Me
   And must follow My teaching.

3. The world will lie in wait for you
   And bring you much mockery and dishonor;
   Will drive you away and outlaw you
   As if Satan were in you.

4. Wenn man euch nun lästert und schmächt,
   Meinethalben verfolgt und schlaegt,
   Seyd froh, denn siehe euer Lohn
   Ist euch bereit ins Himmels Thron.

5. Seht mich an, Ich bin Gottes Sohn,
   Und hab auch allzeit wohl getan,
   Ich bin zwar auch der allerbest,
   Noch habens mich getödt zuletzt.

6. Weil mich die Welt ein bösen Geist
   Und argen Volksverführer heisst,
   Auch meiner Wahrheit widerspricht,
   So wird sie's euch auch schenken nicht.

7. Doch fürcht euch nicht vor solchem Mann,
   Der nur den Leib ertödten kann:
   Sondern fürcht mehr den treuen Gott,
   Der beydes zu verdammen hat.

8. Derselb probiert euch wie das Gold,
   Und ist euch doch als Kindern hold.
   Wo fern ihr bleibt in meiner Lehr,
   Will ich euch lassen nimmermehr.

9. Denn ich bin eu'r und ihr seyd mein,
   Drum wo ich bleib da solt ihr seyn,
   Und wer euch plagt der rührt mein Aug,
   Weh demselben an jenem Tag.

10. Eur Elend, Furcht, Angst, Noth und Pein,
    Wird euch dort grosse Freude seyn,
    Und diese Schand ein Preiss und Ehr
    Wohl vor dem ganzen Himmels Heer.

4. When then you are blasphemed and defamed
   For My sake persecuted and beaten
   Rejoice; for behold your reward
   Is prepared for you at heaven's throne.

5. Behold Me: I am the Son of God
   And have always done the right.
   I am certainly the best of all
   Still they finally killed Me.

6. Because the world calls Me an evil spirit
   And malicious seducer of the people
   And contradicts My truth
   Neither will it go[9] easy with you.

7. Yet fear not such a man
   Who can kill only the body
   But far more fear the faithful God
   Whose it is[10] to condemn both.

8. He it is who tests you as gold
   And yet is loving to you as His children.
   As long as you abide in My teaching
   I will nevermore forsake you.

9. For I am yours and you are Mine
   Thus where I am there shall you be,
   And he who abuses you touches My eye,[11]
   Woe to the same on that day.

10. Your misery, fear, anxiety, distress, and pain
    Will be great joy to you there
    And this shame a praise and honor,
    Yea, before the whole host of heaven.

11. Die Apostel nahmen solches an,
    Und lehrten solch's auch jedermann
    Wer dem Herren nachfolgen wollt,
    Dass er dessen gewarten sollt.

12. O Christe hilf du deinem Volk,
    Welch's dir in aller Treu nachfolgt
    Dass es durch deinen bittern Tod
    Erlöset werd aus aller Noth.

13. Lob sey dir Gott in deinem Thron,
    Darzu auch deinem lieben Sohn;
    Auch dem Heiligen Geist zugleich,
    Der zieh noch viel zu seinem Reich.

11. The apostles accepted this
    And taught the same to everyman;
    He who would follow after the Lord,
    That he should count on as much.

12. O Christ, help Thou Thy people
    Which follows Thee in all faithfulness,
    That though through Thy bitter death
    It may be redeemed from all distress.

13. Praise to Thee, God, on Thy throne
    And also to Thy beloved Son
    And to the Holy Ghost as well.
    May He yet draw many to His kingdom.

If We Now Must Part:[12] A Parting Hymn[13]

Tune: From Psalm 6[14]

Muss Es Nun Seyn Gescheiden

1. Muss es nun seyn gescheiden,
   So woll uns Gott begleiten,
   Ein jedes an sein Ort;
   Da wollend Fleiss ankehren
   Uns'r Leben zu bewähren
   Nach Inhalt Gottes Wort.

2. Das solten wir begehren
   Und nicht hinlässig werden,
   Das End kommt schnell herbey:
   Wir wissen kein morgen,
   Drum lebend doch in Sorgen
   Der G'fahr ist mancherley.

3. Betrachtend wohl die Sachen,
   Dass uns der Herr heisst wachen,
   Zu seyn allzeit bereit:
   Dann so wir würd'n erfunden
   Liegen und schlaf'n in Sünden,
   Es würd uns werden leid.

4. Drum rüstend euch bey Zeiten,
   Und alle Sünd vermeiden
   Lebend in G'rechtigkeit:

If Now Parting It Must Be

1. If now parting it must be,
   May God accompany us
   Each to his place
   There to do his best
   To demonstrate the life we have
   According to what God's Word says.

2. This should we desire
   and not become negligent;
   The end approaches fast;
   We know of no morrow
   Yet still live care-burdened;
   The danger is manifold.

3. Attend well to the matters
   The Lord told us to watch over
   To be always ready;
   For if we were to be found
   Stretched out, asleep in sin
   It were too bad for us.

4. So equip yourself in time
   And shun all sin
   Living in righteousness

Das ist dass rechte Wachen,
Dardurch man mag gerathen
Zur ew'gen Seligkeit.

5. Hiemit seynd Gott befohlen,
Der woll uns allzumahlen,
Durch seine Gnad allein,
Zur ew'gen Freud erheben,
Dass wir nach diesem Leben
Nicht kommen in ewigs Leid.

6. Zum End ist mein Begehren
Denkend meiner im Herren,
Wie ich auch g'sinnet bin:
Nun watchend allesammen,
Durch Jesus Christum, Amen,
Es muss geschieden seyn.

Notes

1. The *Ausband* has ten other hymns attributed to "M.S." but these are generally agreed to be by Michael Schneider, leader of the Passau prisoners' group (*ME*, IV, 470).

2. Above p. 16, note 3: Portions of this hymn appear pp. 229 and 271. Full rhymed versions are given in the appendix of Augsburger's dissertation (above p. 17, note 5) pp. 267 ff.

3. The introduction of numerous additional notes between the original melodic tones is not meant as decoration or aesthetic flourish; it is rather a product of the way the tunes were learned and transmitted over the centuries, especially of the efforts of the *Vorsänger* to lead the congregation as the pace of the singing became ever more slow. A selection of the better-known tunes, as sung in the Kishacoquillas Valley Amish churches, was printed by Joseph W. Yoder, *Amische Lieder*, Huntingdon, Pa., 1942.

4. The evolution of current Amish singing from the sixteenth century origins is analyzed by George Pullen Jackson, "The Strange Music of the Old Order Amish," *The Musical Quarterly*, XXXI, July 1945, pp. 275 ff. An effort to list the known tunes is made in Rosella Reimer Duerksen's *Anabaptist Hymnody of the Sixteenth Century*, unpublished DSM. Thesis, Union Theological Seminary, New York, 1946.

5. According to Duerksen, *op. cit.*, p. 86, the original tune and hymn go back to the seventh or eighth century. In 1535 it appeared in a German translation in a hymnal by Joseph Klug; it is by this German title *Christe der Du bist Tag und Licht* that it is identified in the *Ausbund*. It is used with other Hutterite hymns as well.

6. As the Klug tune is not easy to harmonize with the transcription of J. W. Yoder (*op. cit.*, 31), this alternative tradition as preserved in Anglicanism is also noted

That is true watchfulness
Whereby one can attain
to eternal blessedness.

5. May you hereby be commended to God
   That He would all together
   Through His grace alone
   Raise us to eternal joy
   That we not come after this life
   Into eternal misery.

6. Lastly my desire;
   Remember me in the Lord
   As I too am inclined[15]
   Now be ye all vigilant
   Through Jesus Christ, Amen,
   Parting it must be.

from *Songs of Syon*, ed. G. R. Woodward, London, 1923, p. 211. The second line is much closer to Yoder.

7. *Ausbund* No. 7, p. 46.

8. The narrative style of the beginning seems at first to point to a specific Gospel account, such as Mk. 8:27-38; but then the content of Christ's admonition spreads out much more broadly to include other scriptural allusions as well as other thoughts not in directly scriptural language.

9. "It" is here the "the world," conceived as the agent of persecution, Mt. 10:18, 28; Lk. 12:4 f.

10. I.e., to whom it belongs.

11. Zech. 2:8.

12. *Ausbund* No. 136, p. 791. First printed in 1531 in a Bohemian Brethren hymnal. The association with Sattler goes back to the anthology *Güldene Apffel in Silbern Schalen*, 1702, where it appears (p. 23) just after the Horb letter and the martyrdom account, and in the 17th-century *Sammelband* referred to above p. 5.

13. A *Scheidlied* is a song to be sung at the close of the gathering for worship. Myron S. Augsburger renders it as if it were referring specifically to Sattler's leave-taking with his congregation (*op. cit.* p. 243 and p. 289). Yoder, *op. cit.*, identifies it with the "last Sunday in the year."

14. Duerksen does not identify the "Psalm 6" tune. J. W. Yoder's transcription (p. 9) seems to fit well with the melody of Psalm 6 from Clement Marot's first rhymed (French) psalter of 1542. Marot took its first line from a secular *chanson* rather than from the German. Thus any use of the tune with a German psalm translation must be later than 1542. A text like this would hardly have circulated for over fifteen years without a tune; nor is it very likely that, if used with another from 1527 until after 1542, it would then have shifted to a new Calvinist tune. This would seem to cast doubt on the likelihood of Sattler's authorship.

15. I.e., I will also remember you.

XII

How Scripture
Should Be
Discerningly Exposited

Introduction

The evidence for Michael Sattler's authorship of the present text is limited to the initials "M.S." on the title page. The earliest scholar to link the initials to Sattler was Ludwig Keller;[1] he has been followed with little question by others.[2] There seems to be no record of sixteenth- or seventeenth-century awareness of the tract. Its absence from the *SB* collection and from Van Braght's list of Sattler's works[3] is a testimony against its having been widely used or associated with his memory, but does not count against the presumption of his authorship. A commonality not only of subject matter but of types of argument links this tract to Sattler's branch of Anabaptism. Internal evidence would seem to indicate an origin in the first generation of Anabaptism.

The bulk of the pamphlet is a simple series of New Testament texts, cited in full, with subtitles and glosses serving to point up the sequence of statements. The title's accent on "distinguishing and clarifying" describes the author's concern; to separate the distinct elements of a biblical text in order to accentuate the sequence in which preaching, faith, and baptism are always found.

Such a compendium of texts on baptism was a frequent form of Anabaptist literature. Heinold Fast has set several very early Swiss Brethren texts of this kind in parallel;[4] they testify to the Anabaptist assumptions that (a) the text of

Scripture is self-explanatory when read sincerely, and that (b) the practice of the apostles and the command of Christ are equally valid guides for the Reformation of the church.

Appended to the primary exposition is a brief argument, going slightly beyond the Scripture texts, in response to the equation of circumcision and baptism, one of the standard Reformed arguments for infant baptism. There were other pedobaptist arguments; it is significant that only this one, because of its claimed basis in a distinct scriptural command, was deemed worthy of refutation. This answer leads naturally into two lists of pairs of concepts which illuminate at the same time the relation of Old and New Testament, and the two sides of faith as death and life. These lists have no immediate import for the baptism question. They may very well have existed independently as preaching or teaching outlines before they were added to this leaflet. They serve to illustrate Sattler's predilection for exposition by divisions and distinctions ("how Scriptures may be distinguished and clarified").

This translation diverges only slightly from that published by J. C. Wenger under the title "An Early Anabaptist Tract on Hermeneutics."[5] Since the format is a large part of the point of the pamphlet, we seek to reproduce its peculiarities.

The Text

How Scripture should reasonably
be discerningly exposited
which says of baptism
how the Holy Spirit with His gifts
preceded and follows
and accomplishes His work
first of all
through faith in teaching

1. Teaching	4. Baptism
2. Hearing	5. Spirit
3. Faith	6. Works

Matthew 15 [6]

Every planting which my heavenly Father did not plant, shall be rooted out.

Romans 10

Through the hearing of preaching comes faith.

Acts 2, 8, 9, 10, 16, 18, and 19 [7]

Whoever comes to faith asks to be baptized.

Colossians 2

Beware that no robbery befall you through philosophy and human dogmas.

M.S. [8]

Grace, peace and salvation from God the Father, through the redemption of Christ His beloved Son, through the power and working of His Holy Spirit, Amen.

Old custom which is not true must give way.

Since now so much schism, error and controversy has sprung up, and still springs up daily, the greatest cause of which is that many indolent workers have worked in the Lord's vineyard, who worked sloppily and for the sake of temporal goods, and did not consider that such was necessary, and needed to be done assiduously and earnestly . . . since it brings such harmful danger, namely because of the Ceremonies, which are as far and away from the command and ordinance of the Apostles and Christ as are heaven and earth from one another . . . [9] Then there is still a small difference, what is translated from Latin into German and somewhat distorted, from what the Romish papacy practices. [10] Such as among others

Romish, Lutherish, and Christian are not the same thing.

152

infant baptism, which is from the Popes, their councils and decrees in allegories.[11] Therefore I have had good reason to draw together this work, as follows, so that after all once Scripture is clear before our eyes, it may be seen, wherein we still might fall short.[12] We need not long debate and dispute, where this or that is commanded or forbidden. Just look here to the plumbline and order, here is the ground of the matter. Why need we argue long about the chrysm, salt, mud, exorcism of devils, godparents, and many more of the same, which have crept in from the Romish church, or perhaps were never done away with.[13] If infant baptism and such ceremonies are grounded in the New Testament, which is here properly exposited, let it be held to assiduously according to Christ's command. But if it is from popes and from men, it should be done away with. All Scripture speaks only of one baptism; which all true Christians (praise God!) recognize. He who seeks it finds it.

One should keep the good and let the evil go.

Christ and Belial do not agree.

How Scripture should reasonably
be distinguished and clarified[14]
which says of baptism
how the Holy Spirit precedes and follows and
confirms His work[15]

The Work[16] of John the Baptist etc.
Mt. 3; Mk. 1; Lk. 3; Jn. 1 and 3

John taught and preached and admonished the people by God's command.

1. First repentance; he reprimanded them for their sin.
2. Second: that they should repent.
3. Third: be baptized for betterment.[17]
4. Fourth: pointed the converts to the kingdom of God.
5. Fifth: pointed with his finger to Jesus the Lamb of God.
6. Sixth: gave a rule to everyone according to his station.[18]
7. Seventh: rebuked the unrepentant Pharisees and others.
8. Eighth: trusted to the wrath and chastisement of God.

John's work

Water baptism
John says: I baptize you with water unto repentance.

Christ's work

Holy Spirit baptism
But he who comes after me will baptize you with fire and the Holy Spirit, Mt. 3; Lk. 3.

Baptism

Water
John baptized with water, Acts 1.

Spirit

Holy Spirit
But you shall be baptized by the Holy Spirit.

Teaching

Teaching
John cried out and said, better yourselves.

Repentance

Repentance
And repent.

*Kingdom of God
manifest*

Kingdom of God
The kingdom of God is at hand

*Hearing
Faith*

Hearing and believing
Then everyone came out to the Jordan to John, and heard John, and the publicans confessed God.[19]

Water

Baptism

And were baptized

Confession

Confession

And confessed their sins

Godless unconverted

The obstinate: does not save.

But the Pharisees and scribes despised the counsel of God against them and did not accept baptism from him: Lk. 7.

Jesus Christ the Living Son of God

first received water baptism from John in the Jordan, Lk. 3.

Water
Spirit

And thereafter the Holy Spirit from His heavenly Father, to fulfill all righteousness.

To Nicodemus Christ says, John 3:

Teaching

Verily, verily I say to you, unless one is born:

Water baptism
Spirit baptism
Is one baptism

Water
of water

Water is mortification
Spirit is quickening

Spirit
and of Spirit,

he cannot enter the kingdom of God.

Teaching

Teaching/faith

Christ taught and preached and imparted faith.

Water

Baptism

His disciples baptized the penitent with water, after teaching.

155

Holy Spirit

Spirit

Christ baptized all whom He had elected and endowed them with His Holy Spirit, Jn. 3 and 4.

What the apostles were to teach
Christ's command, Luke 24

Christ's command

Christ explained to His disciples the Scripture and all understanding, saying, thus the Christ had to suffer, and rise on the third day.

Teaching

Teaching Repentance Forgiveness

And in His name should be preached:
first repentance
and then forgiveness of sin
beginning at Jerusalem.

The Last Command: Matthew 28; Mark 16

Christ's power Disciples' work

Christ spoke to His disciples, all authority is heaven and on earth is given me, go into the whole world.

Teaching

Teaching

Teach all peoples, and preach the gospel to all creatures.

Faith

Faith

He who believes, . . .

Baptism

Baptism

. . . and is baptized, will be saved. Baptize them in the name of the Father, of the Son, and of the Holy Spirit.

Works

Works

. . . and teach them to keep all I have

commanded you. Behold, I am with you unto the end of the world.

Unbelief
Unbelief damns

. . . but he who does not believe will be damned.

Whoever wants to know the teaching should read all the beginnings.[20]
Would be too long to recount everything here.

All passages in the Acts of the Apostles concerning baptism etc.

Repentance and Faith, Acts 2
Repentance
Teaching

Peter spoke to the people, Repent . . .

Water
Obedience

. . . And let everyone be baptized in the name of Jesus Christ for forgiveness of sins. . . .

Promise of the Holy Spirit
Promise

So you shall receive the gift of the Holy Spirit, for it is promised to you and your children.

Faith
Accept teaching

Then those who accepted willingly his word . . .

Water
Being baptized

. . . were baptized and on that day around three thousand souls were added.

Philip converts many in Samaria
Acts of the Apostles 8

Teaching

Teaching
Hearing

Now when the men and women heard Philip preaching . . .

Faith

Faith

. . . they believed in the kingdom of God and the name of Jesus Christ.

Water

Baptism

Then they were baptized, both men and women.

Holy Spirit

Spirit

Peter and John laid their hands on them, and they received the Holy Spirit.

The Eunuch in the Chariot, Acts 8

Teaching

Teaching

Philip said to the Moorish chamberlain, if you believe with all your heart, then it may be.

Faith

Faith

He answered and said, I believe that Jesus Christ is the Son of God.

Water

Baptism

And he commanded the chariot to stop, and went down into the water, Philip together with the chamberlain, and he baptizes him,[21] Acts 8.

Paul's Conversion
Acts 9

Exhortation

Ananias'
exhortation

Ananias said, dear Brother Saul, the Lord who appeared to you on the way, as you came here, has sent me, that you might see again, and be filled with the Holy Spirit. Why do you now hesitate?

Baptism

Paul's
willingness

Arise and be baptized . . .

Spirit

Betterment

And wash away your sins. . . . Acts 22[22]

Prayer

Prayer

And call on the name of the Lord.

Water

Baptism

Then Paul could see again, and arose and was baptized.

Peter converts Cornelius, and many Gentiles to faith, Acts 10

Teaching

Teaching

As Peter was still speaking these words to Cornelius and to the men,

Holy Spirit

Hearing
Faith
Spirit

The Holy Spirit fell upon all those who were listening to the word, and the believers from the circumcision who had come with Peter were astounded, that the gift of the Holy Spirit was also poured out upon Gentiles.

Water

Work of the
servants

Then Peter said, can anyone forbid water, that these should not be baptized, who have received the Holy Spirit just as we did?

Baptism

Baptism

And he ordered that they be baptized in the name of the Lord, Acts 10.

The Purple merchant Lydia, Acts 16

Hearing and Faith

Teaching
Hearing

A God-fearing woman, Lydia by name, a merchant of purple, listened, whose heart the Lord opened, so that she gave heed to what Paul had spoken.

Water

When she and her household were baptized. . . .

Works of Love

She admonished the disciples, saying, if you regard me as believing in the Lord, then enter into my house and dwell there.

The Jailer, Acts 16

His Own Request

The jailer said, dear sirs, what shall I do to be saved?

Teaching and Faith

Paul and Silas said, believe in the Lord Jesus, and you and your house will be saved. They spoke to him the word of the Lord, and to all who were in his house.[23]

Works of Faith

And he took them to his house in the same hour of the night, and washed their stripes.

Water

And he was baptized, with all his household, Acts 16.

Crispus believes with his household and many Corinthians
Acts 18

Teaching and Faith

Paul teaches, and Crispus the head of the School[24] believes in the Lord with his

	entire household, and many Corinthians who were listening believed.
One's own faith	

Water

Baptism	And were baptized, Acts 18.

The Twelve Men at Ephesus
Acts 19

John's Teaching on Repentance and Faith

John's teaching Repentance: Baptism	Paul said to them, John baptized with the baptism of repentance, and said to the people that they should believe in him who was to follow him, that is, in Jesus, the Christ. . . .

Knowledge of Christ and of the Holy Spirit

Paul's teaching Hearing	As they heard this . . .

Water

Rebaptism	They were baptized in the name of the Lord Jesus, Acts 19

Holy Spirit and the Laying on of Hands

Laying on hands	And when Paul laid his hands on them the Holy Spirit came upon them; then they spoke with tongues and prophesied. These twelve men had previously been baptized by Apollos with the baptism of John unto repentance, and are re-baptized by Paul, Acts 18.[25]

Testimony from the Epistles on Baptism
Romans 6

Water: buried in death

Teaching: in baptism sins are buried	Paul says, do you not know that all we who are baptized in Jesus Christ are baptized unto his death? Thus we are buried with him by baptism unto death. Romans 6.

Resurrection in the Spirit

*Faith: in Christ
one rises anew*

So that just as Christ was wakened from the dead by the glory of the Father. . . .

New Life

New Life

. . . we should also walk in new life

Mortifying the Old

Baptism unto death

As we are planted together with him in the same death, . . . Romans 6.

Resurrection of the New

Spirit unto life

So shall we also be like unto the resurrection.

The Function of Apostles and Servants
1 Corinthians 3

*All children must
first believe, then
be baptized*

Who is Paul? Who is Apollos? They are servants, through whom you came to believe, just as the Lord gave to each of them

I planted	i.e., I taught
Apollos watered	i.e., he baptized you
God gave the increase	i.e., the Holy Spirit, whom God sends through Christ

1 Corinthians 6

Water

Teaching:

Paul teaches, saying, You have been washed, . . .

Created by the Father's grace

The Father's mode

You have been sanctified, . . .

Redeemed by Christ the Son

The Son's mode

You have been justified in the name of the Lord Jesus Christ, etc.

Illuminated by the Holy Spirit
And by the Spirit of our God

Colossians 2

Water

*Teaching
Baptism unto death*

Paul teaches, saying, as you are buried with Christ through baptism. . . , Col. 2

Resurrection in the Spirit

Spirit unto life

In whom you also are risen through the faith which God works, who raised him (i.e., Christ)[26] from the dead, Col. 2.

Galatians 3

Water

*Teaching
baptism*

Paul teaches, saying, as many of you as are baptized . . .

New Man in Christ

Spirit

. . . have put on Christ, Gal. 3

Ephesians 4 and 5

Teaching

Paul teaches: One faith, one baptism, one Lord and God, Father of all. Eph. 4

Bath of Water in the Word

*Baptism, letter,
word, is dead*

Paul teaches, saying, and purified them by the bath of water in the Word. Eph. 5

Sanctified in the Spirit

*Spirit
makes alive*

That he might present to himself a church that is glorious, having no spot or wrinkle, or anything of the kind, but that it be holy, irreproachable. Eph 5.

Titus 3

Bath of Water for Re-birth

Teaching

Paul taught, saying, Christ, according to his

Baptism *Death*	mercy, saves us, through the bath of rebirth. . . .
	## Holy Spirit
Spirit *New birth*	And the renewing of the Holy Spirit, which he poured out upon us abundantly, Titus 3.

1 Peter 3

Water and Deluge

Peter's teaching *water is destruction*	In the times of Noah, as the ark was being prepared, in which few, i.e., eight souls, were preserved, through water, the type of [that] which also preserves you:

Baptism

Baptism sanctifies *no one*	Namely baptism, not the putting away of fleshly filth.

Resurrection in a Good Conscience

Conscience *assured by the Spirit*	But the certain testimony of a good conscience with God, through the resurrection of the Lord Jesus Christ, 1 Pet. 3.

1 Corinthians 12 and 15

Spirit

Teaching *Spirit*	Paul teaches, saying in one Spirit we . . .

Water

Water	. . . are all baptized into one body, 1 Cor. 12

Water

Baptism, the *figure of death*	What are they doing who are baptized for the dead, . . . 1 Cor. 15.

Resurrection
. . . if indeed the dead are not to rise?

The danger of baptism

*By the Spirit
one is raised*

Why are they baptized for the dead, and why would we be in hourly danger for our boasting . . . read the entire chapter on the resurrection.

From the tenth chapter to the Hebrews

The Power of Faith

*Teaching
Faith*

So let us approach him with sincere hearts and entire faith.

The Strength of the Spirit

*Assured in
the Spirit*

Sprinkled in our hearts and freed from the evil conscience,

The Work of the Water

Baptism an aid

Our bodies washed with pure water.

Proper Walk

Proper works

Let us hold to the confession of hope, and not waver, for he is faithful, who has promised it. Heb. 10.

In 1 John 5

Three things testify in heaven

1. The Father		1. God
2. The Word	means	2. Man
3. and the Holy Spirit		3. Spirit

Three testify on earth

1. The Spirit		1. Spirit
2. Water	means	2. Baptism
3. and Blood		3. Cross

And the three serve as one

Paul says, Colossians 2

Warning

Let no one take away your prize, who goes about according to his own choice, etc. [27]

These texts are most briefly indicated. The long preceding teachings and words I have let stand, so that not much would be left but what is needed here.[28] He who wants to read everything from the beginning, how the teaching of such things is lengthily introduced, may do so. The teaching of faith always precedes baptism and everything else. For Paul

Romans 10

says, from hearing preaching comes faith.

The Deluge Is a True Figure of Baptism and Not Circumcision

Witness: 1 Peter 3

Peter says, Since Christ also suffered once for our sins, the righteous for the unrighteous, that he might lead us to God, and was put to death according to the flesh, but made alive according to the Spirit; in the same Spirit he also went to preach to the spirits in prison, which were unbelieving aforetimes, while awaiting

Gen. 6
Luke 17

the patience, at the time of Noah, when the ark was prepared, in which a few, *i.e.,* eight souls were preserved through water, which is the figure of what saves you, namely baptism, not the removal of the filth of the flesh, but the certain assurance of a good conscience with God, by the resurrection of Jesus Christ, who has

Note: the
deluge is the figure

ascended to the right hand of God in heaven.

Circumcision Is an Example and Figure
of the Purification of the Heart

Scriptural Testimony from
the Old Testament

Deut. 10

Moses spoke to the people of Israel at God's command; circumcise your hearts, and be no longer stiff-necked, for the Lord your God is God of gods and Lord of lords.

Further

Deut. 30

And the Lord your God will circumcise your heart and the heart of your seed, so that you will love the Lord your God with your whole heart and your whole soul, that you might live.

Jeremiah on the Circumcision
of the Hearts: Chap. 4

Jer. 4

So the Lord speaks to those in Judah and Jerusalem: plow a new furrow and sow not under the hedges. Circumcise yourselves unto the Lord, do away the foreskin of your hearts, men of Judah and people of Jerusalem.

Further

Jer. 6

Ah! with whom should I speak and testify, that someone might hear! But their ears are uncircumcised; they cannot hear.

Further

Jer. 9

Behold, the time comes, says the Lord, when I will visit all the circumcised as well as the uncircumcised, namely Egypt,

Judah, Edom, the children of Ammon, Moab and all who live in the desert places, for all the heathen have uncircumcised foreskins, but the whole house of Israel has uncircumcised hearts.

Circumcision Is a Figure of the Purification of the Heart, Which Paul Calls Circumcision Without Hands

Witness of the New Testament

Acts 6, 7

Stephen reprimands the obstinate Jews in the Council, who blasphemed and persecuted the Word of God, saying to them: you stiff-necked people, uncircumcised in heart and ears, you always strive against the Holy Spirit; as did your fathers, so you also do.

Rom. 2

Paul says; he is not a Jew, who is a Jew outwardly. Nor is circumcision what is done outwardly to the flesh. Rather he is a Jew who is inwardly hidden;[29] the circumcision of the heart takes place in the spirit, not in the letter. Its praise is not from men, but from God.

Further

Phil. 3

Paul says, Philippians 3, We are the circumcision who serve God in the Spirit, and boast of Christ Jesus, and find no consolation in the flesh.

Further

Col. 2

Paul says, Colossians 2, Watch lest anyone rob you through philosophy, and vain seduction according to the principles of men, and of the world, and not according to Christ; for in him dwells the entire fullness of the Deity essentially, and you are filled with the same, who is the head of all principality and authority, in whom you also are circumcised with the circumcision without hands, by the laying off of the sinful body of flesh.

Further

In Christ Jesus neither circumcision nor uncircumcision counts, but a new creature.[30]

Summa on Circumcision

Gen. 15

God instituted circumcision in the Old Testament with Abraham and his seed, so that infant boys should be circumcised on the eighth day. Whoever was not circumcised, his soul should be removed from his people. Thus came the covenant of God, which He Himself offered to His people, that under this sign, in obedience, they should be elect from among all peoples. Yet it was sometimes suspended, as during the forty years in the desert, and as long as the Babylonian captivity lasted, and as often as the people suffered great distress, with reason.[31] And finally [it was] fully abolished by the prophets and judged impotent.

Josh. 5
Read the books Ezra, Nehemiah & Maccabees

Second, circumcision cannot be an analogy to baptism; if it were, one would have to observe exactly the eighth day, and God would have to coerce us too with threatening.[32] And Christ would have had

*Christ forces
no one into baptism*

to have Himself baptized in His infancy, for He must have known well what baptism is and means, something other children cannot know. And one should not baptize the little girls, for they were not circumcised; the law does not apply to them as to the boys. And the rule would need to remain after the translation.[33] Whatever infant boy is not baptized on the eighth day, his soul shall be rooted out, or damned. The child baptizers press circumcision hard and how baptism is supposed to be instituted in its place, but they have not so much as a dot in all Scripture; as little as they have for godparenthood, or that it were said: "baptize the infants as soon as they leave the mother's womb."

Wherefore baptizing little children, godparenthood, exorcism, chrysm, oils, salt, mud, are all together vain, notions of men, without command of Christ or apostolic usage. Therefore let one be on guard against them!!

Father	**Son**	**Holy Spirit**

Baptism in water and in the Holy Spirit: one baptism, but two natures and properties, as follows

Unto death: Water	**Unto life: Spirit**
The way to repentance	New life
To the destruction of sin	A good walk
Drowning iniquity	In the Spirit's power
Taking reason captive	Firm faith
Losing self-will	Ardent love

Mortifying the old Adam	Constant hope
Death's door	Good works[34]
Renouncing the devil	Persistent truth
Laying aside evil lusts	Constant righteousness
Works changeable	Unwavering disposition
Rejecting the world	Steadfast patience
Hating oneself	Perseverance in peace
Burial in death	Risen and walking with Christ
Nullifying the flesh	With Him doing the Father's will
Suppressing vices	Recognizing the Father in Him
Losing of one's first life	Keeping His word
Descending to hell	Loving one's enemy from the heart
Enduring God's judgment	Feeding the hungry
Not demanding justice	Giving the thirsty to drink
Willingly bearing vengeance and reproach	Clothing the naked
Loving contrary to nature	Visiting the sick and prisoners
Desiring contrary to the flesh	Sheltering strangers
Seeking condemnation	Sober, chaste, moderate
Rejoicing in reproach, mockery, and shame	Persevering to the end
Being the world's fool	In sum: everything good in God
The devils' footstool	Illumined, preserved, endowed
Despairing of oneself[35]	with the Holy Spirit by pure
In Sum: overcoming all patiently	grace unto an eternal life of blessedness, Amen.
	Without me you can do nothing.
	John 14

This is: to bear the cross

Was	**Take Note**[36]	**That**
The old man		The new man
Moses, the Law		Christ, grace
Curse		Blessing
Sin		Righteousness
Death		Life

Doubt	Faith
Enmity	Love
Desperate	Hope[37]
Blasphemy	Innocence
Damnation	Blessedness
Disobedience	Discipline
Blindness	Insight
Lies	Truth
Pride	Humility
Avarice	Thankful
Envy	Patience
Unchaste	Purity
Gluttony	Sober
Wrath	Benevolence
Punishment	Mercy
Mourning	Joy
Care	Consolation
Anxiety	Rest
Unmindful	Attentive
Distress	Peace
Torment	Released
Instinct	Sincere
Nothingness	Everything
Servitude	Sonship
Vain	Content
Laziness	Watchful
False	Correct
Inconstant	Constant
Shame	Praise
Vengeance	Pardon
Foolishness	Wisdom
Abrupt	Mild
Loss	Gain
Spiritless	Spirited
Death	Life
Flesh	Spirit
Night	Day

Darkness	Light
Yesterday	Today
Downfall	Resurrection
Hell	Heaven
Evil	Good
No	Yes
Devil	Angel
Cross	Honor

The earthly Adam ruined and lost everything. In sum: through the instigation and the envy of the devil death came into the whole world. Wisdom 2.

The heavenly Adam restored everything and sanctified it by His Holy Spirit which goes out from the Father to all newborn men; John 3; 1 Cor. 15

Conclusion

If we would properly train and prepare ourselves for a repentant life, beginning first with ourselves, and would fervently perceive the will of God, then all contention, envy, hatred, pride, and whatever hinders us from following Christ would indeed fade away. If each were to search his own heart, he would be so aghast, that he would let everything else go, and would busy himself with true repentance, would search himself out, and ask after the will of God, and shun all teachings of men and vanity of this world, and hold firmly to God's Word, and prove with brotherly love what it teaches, leading to self-knowledge those who are in error.[38] Now he who presents himself to the Lord Christ, [ready] for all obedience and for the discipline and admonition of the Holy Spirit, will

Ps. 139
Acts 9
Col. 2
Eccles. 3
1 Cor. 13
Jas. 2
Mt. 11

soon find a Peter, Paul, Ananias, Apollos, a servant of God and brother of the fellow believers, so that he might not remain in error, and so that on that day he will have no excuse to plead. For many kings, princes, and mighty ones have desired to hear, see, and receive what we have seen, heard, and received in this last time. Noah was a solitary man preaching repentance, who could not yet preach the things which we now have received in Christ. Therefore it will be more tolerable for the former world than for the latter. Had Sodom and Gomorrah seen and heard such things as we, they would still stand, for they would have repented. The Queen of Sheba traveled far and wide to hear Solomon's wisdom, and we have now received much more from God. The Wise Men also came a long way to Bethlehem to worship Christ. When Jonah preached repentance in Nineveh and they heard of the wrath of God, the king was converted together with the whole city, and cattle and men repented. It will also be more tolerable for Jerusalem, Judah, Samaria, Capernaum, yea, even for the heathen Tyre and Sidon, than for this last world, of it does not repent. For the ax is already laid at the foot of the tree. The tree that bears no good fruit will be chopped off and thrown into the fire. Christ will also purge His threshing floor; He has the winnowing fan already in His hand. Therefore let him flee who can, under the mighty hand of God, and let him accept chastisement, and no longer strive against the truth, for it is known and the wisdom of God must be vindicated by her children in the streets, that the last state may not be worse than the first. Therefore let

Mt. 13

Gen. 6
2 Pet. 2
Gen. 19
Mt. 12
1 Kg. 10

Mt. 2
Jonah 2, 3
Mt. 12

Mt. 3
Lk. 3

2 Tim. 2
Mt. 11
and 12

174

Lk. 10

every one be warned and may he pray God from the heart for the blessedness he lacks. Let him seek it with humble heart at the feet of Christ, like Mary, and preserve it with all diligence; let him keep himself from restlessness, busyness, human opinions, and vain effort; for thereby no burdened heart can find peace. For

Lk. 24
Phil. 3
Heb. 7, 9
Mt. 17

all human teaching is forbidden, for Christ Himself ordered everything rightly, according to the command of the Father; for which cause He came to earth and paid everything with His blood. Him alone we would hear. To Him alone be eternal glory, praise, and honor, with the Father, in the Holy Spirit. Amen.

Notes

1. *Allgemeine Deutsche Biographie*, XXX, 412.

2. Hans Joachim Hillerbrand, *A Bibliography of Anabaptism, 1529-1630*, No. 2757, p. 126.

3. T. J. van Braght, *The Bloody Theatre or Martyr's Mirror*, Elkhart, Indiana, 1886, p. 405.

4. Fast, "Hans Krüsis Büchlein," in *A Legacy of Faith*, C. J. Dyck, editor, 1962, pp. 213 ff., especially pp. 225 and 256.

5. *MQR*, Vol. XLIII, Jan. 1969, pp. 26 ff.

6. This text from Mt. 15 was the watchword of the radical Reformation: it distinguishes Zwingli and his followers from the less sweeping programs of the Anglican and Lutheran Reformers. Whereas they were ready to reject any elements of the Catholic heritage which Scripture forbade, Zwingli sought to ban all that Scripture did not command. Cf. *Ratschläge betreffend Messe und Bilder, Z*, II. p. 808.

7. Whereas the other text references are direct quotations, the references to Acts are to a constant characteristic of the baptism narratives.

8. The initials "M.S." conclude the title page; the following Preface likewise occupies one full page.

9. The translation preserves the unclear syntax of the original; everything up to this point is one complex sentence. "That such was necessary" refers back to "work in the Lord's vineyard"; the source of the "harmful danger" is the "schism, error, and controversy"; the two themes of decay and renewal intertwine in the sentence without the grammatical relationships always being clear.

10. The author shows an awareness of history and cultural change, which would fit well with Sattler's Benedictine background. The standard Roman Catholic practice, he says, is far from the New Testament standards; the transition to Germanic culture makes the distance even a little greater.

11. That "infant baptism is from the popes" was a standard Swiss Brethren statement. "Pope" is here a symbol of apostate religion: the statement can be made without

175

any need to document which pope introduced the usage. Yet the earliest Zürich brothers did develop an interpretation of the liturgical history: Yoder, *Gespräche*, p. 18.

12. This language testifies to an early point in the development of the Reformation. "We still fall short" places the author with the readers in the concern to finish an incomplete Reformation. There are no fixed, named debating positions, Anabaptist or others, as there are in *Brotherly Union*, see p. 35 and *Letter to Horb*, see p. 73 above. The freshness of the author's trust in the purifying effect of the return to Scripture is unshadowed by the experience of persecution and apostasy. The degeneracy of the present state of the church is due to lazy clergy, not to the machinations of the devil. All of this would support an origin as early as Sattler's 1526 ministry.

13. Here the author looks back on a few years of beginning Reformation, during which practices once rejected in principle could have "crept back in," or during which there would have been time to do away with them; 1519-26 would suffice for such a view.

14. Following the preface, the text proper begins on p. Aii with the reiteration of the title. It would seem at first that "Scripture" means the Bible and that the author is promising a general treatise on biblical interpretation (cf. the title chosen by J. C. Wenger for his translation). But the relative "which says . . ." restricts the noun. The title promises to deal only with "Scripture on baptism." The key to interpretation is "distinguishing"; the later text itself explains what this means: finding patterns, sequences, steps.

15. This particular phrasing, that "the Holy Spirit precedes and follows and confirms," does not recur as such in the book; yet it capsules the author's view of the entire event of faith. The proper work of the Holy Spirit is faith (cf. title page: "first of all through faith in teaching"). But this is *preceded* by the Spirit's work in proclamation, *followed* in His work of baptism, and *confirmed* by the good works He brings forth.

16. "Work" renders *Ampt*, which might also be translated "function" or "office."

17. "Betterment" is a frequent paraphrase for repentance.

18. Lk. 3:10-14.

19. Cit. "*gaben Gott recht*," i.e., agreed to the rightness of God's judgment. The contrast is direct with the Pharisees' and scribes' attitude later in the same passage.

20. "The teaching" here is the same as "the commandments" in Mt. 28:20. By the "beginnings" which would be "too long to recount" is meant the bulk of Jesus' teachings in the Gospel.

21. The ambiguity of tense is in the original. The author's style of citation wavers between literal repetition and a more lively narrative present.

22. Despite the reference to *Acts 9*, the text cited is 22:16.

23. The advocates of pedobaptism often cited the baptism of households in Acts as evidence that infants might have been included. Sattler accents (note the margin) the claim that each member of the household was instructed.

24. *Schul* is the normal allemanic and yiddish designation for the synagogue.

25. The indication of chap. 18 is a mere typesetting error. The "rebaptism" of the disciples of John in Acts 19 was a standard Anabaptist test case.

26. The parentheses are in the original.

27. Col. 2 is one of Sattler's favorite texts. Cf. above p. 81, note 13. There is a link between the illegitimate preacher's defective message (taking away the prize, or moving the goal) and his defective mandate (being self-appointed).

28. This explanation marks a shift in format. Thus far the texts were quoted in full with a gloss or subtitle for almost every clause: "the long preceding teachings." Henceforth there will be less context cited and less comment made.

29. The reference to Rom. 2:29 would call for: "he is a Jew who is one inwardly."

30. Gal. 6:15. The author or printer omitted the source reference only for this text.

31. What was periodically suspended during Israel's history was not the practice of circumcision, but rather the promise of privilege. The Old Covenant was not withdrawn when the New superseded it: it was already nullified by the later prophets, because of Israel's unfaithfulness.

32. The novelty of baptism as contrasted to circumcision is not so much that the candidate is adult as that he is free.

33. The use of "translation" in this special meaning shows a willingness to debate. Sattler is willing to go along hypothetically for the sake of discussion, in the case for baptism as equated with circumcision; but then one must test the logic with which all the elements of the former practice are "translated" into the forms of the latter.

34. As the list began, the elements on both columns seemed to come in matched pairs, but that is less the case as they go on. Henceforth there is a polarity between the columns as a whole.

35. It may have seemed at first that the left column was evil and the right good, but this would be a misunderstanding, as the last elements in the "water baptism" column confirm. Death is the way to life: the elements in the left column are the prerequisites to the fulfillment on the right. They are not evil, but only inadequate. Cf. the relationship of the two kinds of obedience, above p. 121 and notes 5, and 12.

36. In the original, quadruple columns are used to compress the following lists onto one page. These printed lists are thus different in format and in heading, and therefore presumably in intent, from the earlier pair. Yet there are few clues to the author's precise intention. The heading *was-nota-das* can be variously understood. Earlier (in the analysis of 1 Jn. 5 above) *nota* was a verb or an equation sign, which we translated "means." Elsewhere it is a noun, the name of a very brief document (above p. 135). But here the parallel with *sich* (modern German *siehe*) at the end of the list is decisive; so it must be rendered imperative: "take note." The pronouns are also unclear. *Was* could be interrogative and then *das* would be demonstrative: the old puts a question and the new responds. Yet it is also possible that *was* is a verb (modern German *war*, English "was"), then perhaps *das* should become *dass*, relative particle introducing an affirmation. This ambiguous title is no help in interpreting the document. Its content seems much like the preceding one except that the pairs of terms are logically linked throughout the list. Without speaking directly of baptism or of the pedobaptism controversy, it reinforces the Law/Gospel dialectic, which for the Anabaptists correlates with the movement from the Old Testament to the New, one of the major concerns of Anabaptist hermeneutics.

37. The pairs are most often grammatically equivalent. Yet the author feels free to set a noun in one column against an adjective in the other as long as his point is clear.

38. It is striking that immediately upon accepting new truth for oneself one becomes responsible to share it with others. One's repentance is not focused upon one's own salvation but upon participation in God's reforming work.

Bibliography

Anshelm, Valerius. *Berner Chronik* (5 Bände), K. J. Wyss, Bern, 1896.

Augsburger, Myron. "Michael Sattler, d. 1527, Theologian of the Swiss Brethren Movement," unpublished dissertation, faculty of theology, Union Theological Seminary (Richmond), 1965.

—————. *Pilgrim Aflame.* Herald Press, Scottdale, 1967.

Ausbund. Christoph Saur, Germantown, 1767 (3rd U.S. ed.; many since then).

Bauman, Clarence. *Gewaltlosigkeit im Täufertum.* E. J. Brill, Leiden, 1968.

Beck, Josef. *Die Geschichtsbücher der Wiedertäufer in Oestreich-Ungarn.* . . . Carl Gerold's Sohn, Vienna, 1883.

von Braght, Thieleman Jansz. *The Bloody Theatre or Martyr's Mirror of the Defenceless Christians.* . . . Mennonite Publishing Co., Elkhart, 1886.

Bender, H. S. "Sattler, Michael," *ME*, IV, 1959, p. 427.

—————. "Walking in the Resurrection," *MQR*, XXXV, 2, p. 96.

Blanke, Fritz, "Beobachtungen zum Aeltesten Täuferbekenntnis," *ARG*, XXXVII, 1940, p. 242.

Böhmer, Heinrich. *Urkunden zur Geschichte des Bauernkrieges und der Wiedertäufer.* A. Marcus u. E., Weber, Bonn, 1910. Walter de Gruyter and Co., Berlin, 1933.

Bossert, Gustav. "Sattler, Michael, hervorrangender Täufer Führer," *ML*, IV, 1967, p. 32.

Bullinger, Heinrich. *Vom dern uneuerschapten Fräfel.* . . . Christoffel Froschouer, Zürich, 1531.

Calvin, John. *A Short Instruction for to Arme all Good Christian People Against the Pestiferous Errours of the Common Sect of the Anabaptists.* Jhon Daye, London, 1569.

—————. "Brieve instruction pour armer tous les bons fideles contre les erreurs de la secte commune des Anabaptistes," *CR*, VII, p. 45.

ten Cate, Steven Blaupot. *Geschiedenis der Doopsgezinden in Groningen* I. W. Eekhoff and J. B. Wolters, Leeuwarden and Groningen, 1842.

Clemen, Otto, and Köhler, Walter. *Flugschriften aus den ersten Jahren der Reformation*. (Band I-IV) B. de Craaf, Nieuwkoop, 1967.

[Congregational Order]. State Archive (Bern) UP 80.

Cramer, Samuel, and Pijper, F., ed. "Broederlicke vereeninge von sommighe kinderen Gods," *BRN*, V, 1909, p. 583.

——————. *Het Offer des Herren*. Martinus Nijhoffs, 's Gravenhage, 1904.

——————. "Mennoniten," *RPTK*, XII, 3rd ed., p. 600.

——————. Pijper, F., ed. "Van tweederley ghehoorsaemheyt," *BRN*, V, 1909, p. 633.

Das Evangelium von Jesus Christus in der Welt: Vorträge und Verhandlungen der Sechsten Mennonitschen Weltkonferenz. Verlag Heinrich Schneider, Karlsruhe, 1958.

Duerksen, Rosella Reimer, "Anabaptist Hymnody in the Sixteenth Century," unpublished dissertation, faculty of theology, Union Theological Seminary (New York), 1946.

Dumont, Maurice. "Les Anabaptistes en Pays Neuchatelois," licentiate thesis, faculty of theology, Neuchatel, 1937.

Dyck, C. J., ed. *A Legacy of Faith*. Faith and Life Press, Newton, 1962.

Fast, Heinold. *Der Linke Flügel der Reformation;* Klassiker des Protestantismes, Band IV, Sammlung Dietrich, Carl Schunnemann Verlag, Bremen, 1962.

——————. "Die Sonderstellung der Täufer in St. Gallen und Appenzell," *Z*, XI, 1960, p. 223.

Fast, Heinold, and Yoder, J. H. "How to Deal with Anabaptists: an Unpublished Letter of Heinrich Bullinger," *MQR*, XXXIII, 2, p. 83.

Fellmann, Walter, ed. *Hans Denck: Schriften* (Teil II). C. Bertelsmann Verlag, Gütersloh, 1959.

Ferm, Robert L. *Readings in the History of Christian Thought,* Holt, Rinehart, Winston, New York, 1964.

Fosdick, Harry Emerson. *Great Voices of the Reformation*. Random House, New York, 1912.

Friedmann, Robert, "The Oldest Church Discipline of the Anabaptists," *MQR*, XXIX, 2, p. 162.

——————. "The Schleitheim Confession (1527) and other doctrinal writings of the Swiss Brethren in a hitherto unknown edition," *MQR*, XVI, 2, p. 82.

——————. "Schneider, Michael," *ME*, IV, 1959, p. 470.

Franz, Günther, and Köhler, Walter. *Wiedertäuferakten, 1527-1626,* Band IV of *Urkundliche Quellen zur hessischen Reformations-*

geschichte. N. G. Elwertsche Verlags Buchhandlung, Marburg, 1951.

Füsslin, Johann Konrad. *Beytrage zur Erläuterung der Kirchenreformationsgeschichte des Schweitzerlands* (Band II). Zürich, Conrad Orell, 1741.

Geiser, Samuel, "Lingg," *ME*, III, 1957, p. 350.

Gerbert, Camill. *Geschichte der Strassburger Sektenbewegung zur Zeit der Reformation 1524-1534.* Heitz u. Mündell, Strasbourg, 1889.

Goeters, J. F. Gerhard. *Ludwig Hätzer, Spiritualist und Antitrinitäter.* C. Bertelsmann Verlag, Gütersloh, 1957.

Graber, J. D. "Divorce," *ME*, II, 1956, p. 74.

Gratz, Delbert. *Bernese Anabaptists.* Herald Press, Scottdale, 1953.

Güldene Aepffel in Silbern Schalen . . ." n.p., 1702.

Hillerbrand, Hans J. "The Anabaptist View of the State," *MQR*, XXXIII, 2, p. 83.

Hillerbrand, Hans-Joachim. *A Bibliography of Anabaptism 1529-1630.* No. 2757, Institute of Mennonite Studies, Elkhart, 1962.

—————. *Die Politische Ethik des Oberdeutschen Täufertums.* E. J. Brill, Leiden/Köln, 1962.

Hulshof, Abraham, *Geschiedenis van de Doopsgezinden te Straatsburg von 1525-1557.* J. Clausen, Amsterdam, 1905.

Jackson, George Pullen. "The Strange Music of the Old Order Amish," *The Musical Quarterly*, XXXI, 3, p. 275.

Jackson, S. M., trans. *Selected Works of Huldreich Zwingli.* University of Pennsylvania Press, Philadelphia, 1901.

Jenny, Beatrice. *Das Schleitheimer Taufbekenntnis.* Kark Augustin Verlag, Thayngen, 1951.

Kiwiet, Jan. *Pilgrim Marpeck.* J. G. Oncken, Kassel, 1957.

Krebs, Manfred, and Rott, Hans Georg. *Quellen zur Geschichte der Täufer.* Elsass I, Band VIII (1960), Gerd Mohn, Gütersloh.

Künzli, Edwin, ed. *Huldreich Zwingli: Auswahl seiner Schriften.* Zwingli Verlag, Zürich, 1962.

Leith, John H. *Creeds of the Church.* Doubleday, Garden City, 1963.

Lumpkin, Wm. *Baptist Confessions of Faith.* Judson Press, Chicago, 1959.

McGlothlin, W. J. *Baptist Confessions of Faith.* American Baptist Publication Society, Philadelphia, 1911.

Meihuizen, H. W. "The Concept of Restitution in the Anabaptism of Northwestern Europe," *MQR*, XLIV, 2, p. 149.

—————. "Who were the 'False Brethren' mentioned in the Schleitheim Articles?" *MQR*, XLI, 3, p. 200.

Müller, Ernst. *Geschichte der Bernischen Täufer.* J. Huber, Frauenfeld, 1895.

Müller, Lydia. *Glaubenszeugnisse Oberdeutscher Taufgesinnten.* Band XX of *Quellen und Forschungen zur Reformations-geschichte.* M. Heinsius Nachfolger, Leipzig, 1938.

Pletscher, Werner. "Wo entstand das Bekenntnis von 1527?" *MGB,* V, 1940, p. 20.

[Sammelband] Concordanz und Zeiger der Nahmhaftigsten Sprüch aller Biblischen Bücher . . . Mennonite Historical Library (Goshen).

Seguy, Jean. "Les trois plus anciennes disciplines de l' Anabaptisme," *Christ Seul,* Jan. 1967, p. 13, Feb. 1967, p. 5.

Stauffer, Ethelbert. "The Anabaptist Theology of Martyrdom," *MQR,* XIX, 3, p. 179.

Stayer, James M. "The Doctrine of the Sword in the First Decade of Anabaptism," unpublished dissertation, Cornell University, 1964.

Stupperich, Robert. *Martin Bucers Deutsche Schriften.* Band I (1960), Band II (1962), Gerd Mohn, Gütersloh/Presses Universitaire de France, Paris.

Wenger, J. C. "Brüderlich Vereinigung," *ME,* I, 1955, p. 447.

―――――――. trans. "Concerning Divorce. . . ," *MQR,* XXI, 2, p. 114.

―――――――. trans. "Concerning the Satisfaction of Christ. . . ," *MQR,* XX, 4, p. 243.

―――――――. *Doctrines of the Mennonites.* Mennonite Publishing House, Scottdale, 1952.

―――――――. trans. "An Early Anabaptist Tract on Hermeneutics," *MQR,* XLIII, 1, p. 26.

―――――――. trans. "Martin Weinger's Vindication of Anabaptism, 1935," *MQR,* XXII, 3, p. 180.

―――――――. trans. "The Schleitheim Confession of Faith," *MQR,* XIX, 4, p. 244.

―――――――. trans. "Two Kinds of Obedience. . . ," *MQR,* XXI, 1, p. 18.

Westin, Gunnar, and Bergston, Torsten, et al. *Balthasar Hubmaier: Schriften.* C. Bertelsmann, Gütersloh, 1962.

Widmer, Pierre, and Yoder, John, *Principes et Doctrines Mennonites.* Publications Mennonites, Brussels and Montebeliard, 1955.

Williams, George H. *The Radical Reformation.* Westminster Press, Philadelphia, 1962.

Williams, George H., and Mergal, A. *Spiritual and Anabaptist Writers* LCC, Vol. XXV, Westminster Press, Philadelphia, 1957, p. 21.

Wiswedel, Wilhelm, *Bilder und Führergestalten aus dem Täufertum ein Beitrag zur Reformationsgeschichte des 16 Jahrhunderts.* Vol. III, J. G. Oncken, Kassel, 1952.

Wolkan, Rudolf, *Geschichtsbuch der Hutterischen Brüder.* Carl

Fromme, Vienna, 1923.

Woodward, G. R., ed. *Songs of Syon.* n.p., London, 1923.

Yoder, J. H. "Balthasar Hubmaier and the Beginnings of Swiss Anabaptism," *MQR*, XXXIII, 1, p. 5.

——————. "Binding and Loosing," *Concern* 14, 1967, p. 15.

——————. *Die Gespräche Zwischen Täufern und Reformatoren in der Schweitz 1523-1538.* H. Schneider, Karlsruhe, 1962.

——————. *Täufertum und Reformation in Gespräch.* Basler Studien, Band 13, EVZ Verlag, Zürich, 1968.

Yoder, Joseph. *Amische Lieder.* Yoder Publishing Co., Huntingdon, 1942.

Zieglschmid, A. J. F., ed. *Die Aelteste Chronik der Hutterischen Brüder.* Carl Schurz Memorial Foundation [Philadelphia], 1943.

Zwingli, Huldreich. "Contra Catabaptistarum Strophas Elenchus," Z, VI, p. 106.

——————. "Ratschläge betreffend Messe und Bilder," Z, II, p. 808.

——————. "Wer Ursache gibt zu Aufruhr," Z, III, 1914, p. 374.

——————. "Zwingli an Haller u. Kolb," Z, IX, 1925, p. 108.

Index

Index of Persons

Index of Concepts and Titles

Index of Scripture References